First published in 2009 by Conran Octopus Ltd,
a part of Octopus Publishing Group,
2–4 Heron Quays, London E14 4JP
www.octopusbooks.co.uk

An Hachette Livre UK Company
www.hachettelivre.co.uk

Distributed in the United States and Canada by Hachette Book Group USA,
237 Park Avenue, New York, NY 10017 USA

British Library Cataloguing-in-Publication Data.
A catalogue record for this book is available from the British Library.

Publisher: Lorraine Dickey
Chief Contributor: John Wainwright
Managing Editor: Sybella Marlow
Copy Editor: Alison Wormleighton

Art Direction and Design: Jonathan Christie
Photography: Nick Pope
Picture Researcher: Anne-Marie Hoines

Production Manager: Katherine Hockley

ISBN: 978 1 84091 523 5
Printed and bound in China

CHAIRS

JUDITH MILLER

CHAIR PORTRAITS BY NICK POPE

Contents

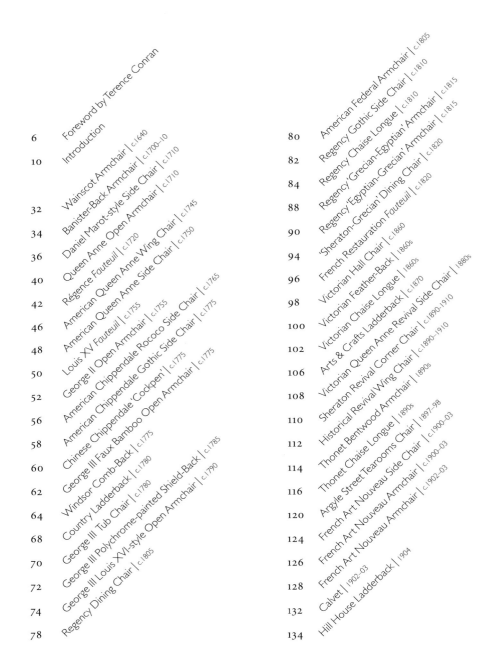

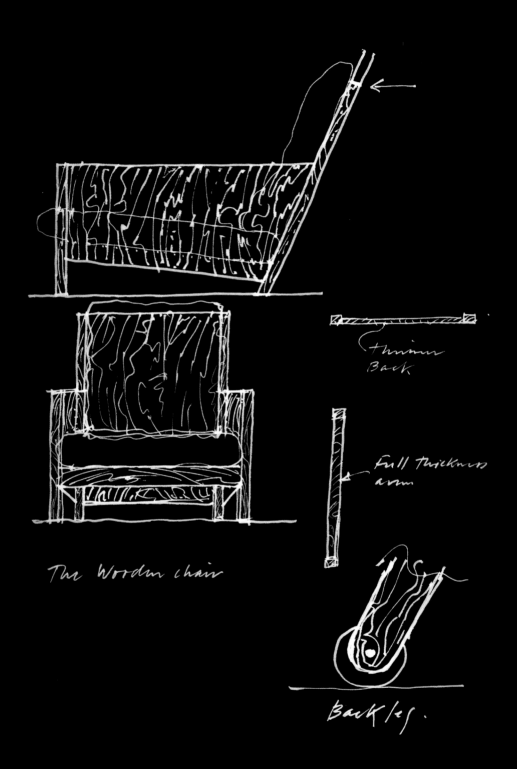

Thinner Back

Full thickness arm

The Wooden chair

Back less.

Foreword
by Terence Conran

Chairs are not just for sitting on, and many are diabolically uncomfortable because their designers have ignored the basic principles of ergonomics. To me this is unintelligent design. A lot of chairs have become indoor sculpture, and in many cases the architects who have designed them have promoted their brand through the design of their chairs – for example, Corbusier, Saarinen, Eames, Alvar Aalto, Gio Ponti, Arne Jacobsen, Marcel Breuer and Mies van der Rohe. Certainly the general public are more aware of their chair designs than their architecture. Sometimes I think that you are unlikely to be a successful architect or designer unless you have designed a classic chair, and this is not just a contemporary phenomenon.

I'm sure that somebody could write a book about the personality and psychology of chairs that describes what sort of person you are by the chairs you would like to acquire, and which would help to indicate how well you will get on with your future husband or wife when you choose the chairs for the marital home. You may, however, prefer to live chairless in sin.

To me a good chair must be elegant and beautiful to look at, easy to move, well made, comfortable to sit in, good for your posture, affordable and durable. I'm glad to say that most of the huge parade of chairs in this excellent book achieve these criteria – but Thonet still remains *my* hero.

Left
The wooden club chair, designed by Terence Conran, is a deeply comfortable and contemporary take on a traditional club chair, with solid ash sides and down-filled chocolate leather upholstery.

Introduction

In Western culture the definition of a chair is a seat with a back designed for a single person. This differentiates it from a stool, which is backless, and also from benches, settees and other forms of elongated seating intended to support more than one individual. Chairs are invariably raised above the ground, usually but not always on legs, and are also movable.

Ancient Egypt

The earliest well-documented use of chairs was in ancient Egypt. Hieroglyphics and wall paintings date them to the Old Kingdom of c.2686–2134BCE. However, a complex set of beliefs regarding the afterlife, which resulted in ceremonial and household furniture being sealed in the burial chambers of Egyptian Pharaohs and other dignitaries, also ensured the physical survival of a number of stools and chairs from this period – the preservation of their wooden components being equally owing to Egypt's very dry climate. One of the best-known examples is a wooden armchair with carved animal legs and paw feet, discovered in 1925 in the tomb of Queen Hetepheres, who died c.2589–2566BCE during the reign of her son, the Pharaoh Khufu. The other, discovered by Howard Carter in 1922, is the golden throne of Tutankhamun. Of more recent origin (c.1334–1325BCE), it has a carved wooden frame covered in sheet gold and silver, inlaid with semi-precious stones, and polychrome painted. Carved imagery includes lion heads and paws, ducks, winged serpents and, on the back panel, Tutankhamun seated on a throne as his wife, Ankhesenamun, applies oils to his arms.

While the most common form of seating in ancient Egypt was the stool – either three- or four-legged, or with a folding X-frame – Tutankhamun's throne reveals just how advanced Egyptian chair-making became during the second millennium BCE. Working with indigenous woods such as sycamore and acacia, as well as imported timbers such as Lebanese cedar and ebony, Egyptian craftsmen developed sophisticated forms of construction – notably peg, dovetail and mortise-and-tenon joints – that have been in use almost ever since. To these can be added decorative techniques such as the masking of poor-quality woods or rough joints with veneers, *gesso* or paint; elaborate *in situ* or applied carving; inlay work with exotic timbers, ivory, bone, precious metals and semiprecious stones; and gilding, with gold and silver leaf.

The rich Egyptian legacy of chair-making techniques – which also included basic upholstery devices such as woven-cord matting, animal-hide seats and rush- and feather-stuffed cushions – was augmented by a vocabulary of ornament that would prove equally inspirational to subsequent cultures and ages. Favoured forms were zoomorphic chair legs and arms modelled on lions, bulls, gazelles, ducks and geese. Other prominent carved or painted imagery included sphinxes, gods (notably the jackal-headed Anubis), scarabs, winged serpents, winged discs or globes (associated with the deity Horus, and a symbol of protection in earthly and eternal life), and plant forms such as lotus flowers and daisies.

Left
Discovered in 1922, in the tomb of the Egyptian Pharaoh Tutankhamun, this carved, gilded, bejewelled and polychrome painted throne dates to around c.1334–1325BCE.

Ancient Greece

Ancient texts refer to the use of stools and chairs in the Minoan civilization centred on the island of Crete, c.2700–1450BCE and also the larger Mycenaean civilization that superseded it, c.1600–1100BCE, on the mainland and islands of what later became Greece. For example, impressive-sounding Mycenaean chairs made of ebony and inlaid with gold and ivory are specifically mentioned. Sadly, however, the demise of Mycenaean civilization – the result of Dorian military invasion, earthquakes and climate change – means that neither physical examples nor visual records have survived. Fortunately, this is in marked contrast to the substantial legacy of the Archaic, or Early, Greek civilization of c.750–480BCE and the Classical Greek era, which immediately followed it and ended with the death of Alexander the Great in 323BCE. As with the Minoan and Mycenaean cultures, few physical examples of stools and chairs from these periods survive. They are, however, well represented in literature, painting, sculpture and ceramics.

Egyptian influence is immediately evident in the most common form of Greek seating: the stool. The two basic models were the *diphros*, which had a flat rectangular seat raised on three or four legs, and the *diphros okladias*, a development of the Egyptian folding X-frame stool. When folded it was easily transportable. Depending on the status of its owner, it varied considerably in its degree of ornamentation, ranging from plain wood to versions with soft leather seats, carved animal legs, inlay work and precious metal hoof or paw feet.

Even the grandest stools did not, however, have the status of the *thronos* (throne). These were the seats of gods – Zeus is depicted on the Parthenon frieze in a *thronos* raised on animal feet and decorated with winged sphinxes – and were associated with heads of state. Otherwise, their use was largely confined to the wealthiest of households and to seats of honour at public gatherings. Many early wooden examples are similar to Egyptian models with animal legs and feet, while others are raised more simply on turned or rectangular-section legs. Most imposing, however, were the *thronai* with solid sides and curved or rectangular backs carved from marble or other stone. The best-known surviving example is the Athenian Elgin Throne, carved from Hymettian marble and dating from the 4th century BCE.

By far the most innovative Greek chair, however, was the *klismos*. Most were made from wood, notably olive and cedar, and some from bronze. Although there were stylistic variations, the basic form comprised a flat-fronted seat with flat or curved sides, secured on four outwardly curved and splayed, sabre-like legs. Rising up from the back legs and the back of the seat, a curved splat tapered up to a curved back rest; in some versions a pair of arms S-curved down from the back rest to the front sides of the seat, while others were armless. Although they almost invariably terminated in plain rather than paw, claw or hoof feet, other decorative embellishments ranged from none at all to exotic silver, ivory or tortoiseshell inlay, gilding, carving and painting.

Sophisticated construction, utilizing mortise-and-tenon joints and probably steamed bentwood for the back, was accompanied in the supportive and comfortable *klismos* by a lightness and sweeping elegance of form. They ensured the chair's contemporary and enduring popularity, which was most evident in the revival of Greek style under the banner of Neo-Classicism during the late 18th and early 19th centuries. To that specific inheritance can also be added a significant vocabulary of decoration. Carved or painted plant forms included rosettes,

Top left
The gravestone (or *stele*) of an Athenian shoemaker, Xanthippos, is dated to c.430BCE and depicts him seated on a *klismos*.

Bottom left
Carved from Hymettian marble, the imposing Elgin throne is Athenian, from the 4th century BCE, and of a type often employed as a seat of honour at public gatherings.

wreaths, festoons of flowers, acanthus leaves and anthemia, while prominent animal imagery included rams, oxen, bulls, goats, horses and the skulls of sacrificial animals. Other prominent decorative devices included vases, urns, medallions depicting gods, goddesses and their attendants, and various geometric designs, notably Greek key patterns.

Ancient and Imperial Rome

From its foundation as a city c.750BCE, through its development as the heart of a kingdom and then a republic, Rome gradually adopted many of the Egyptian and Grecian forms of seating. The process of acquisition, and of adaptation, rapidly accelerated once both Egypt and Greece were subjugated after the formal establishment of the Roman Empire, c.30BCE. While most Roman seating was made of wood and therefore has not survived the passage of time, a fair number of pieces carved from marble or limestone, or cast and forged from bronze, copper or iron, have endured. Combined with visual records in surviving Roman carvings, wall paintings and painted ceramics, they have constituted a well-documented source of inspiration for revivals and re-interpretations of Roman-style seating from the Renaissance onwards.

As in Egypt and Greece, the stool was commonly used, with the most notable of many variants being a substantial four-legged version of the Greek *diphros* and a prestigious X-frame folding stool known as a *sella curulis*. Employed by senators and senior magistrates, the latter could be highly ornate. Some iron-legged models, for example, had plant-form decoration inlaid in gold, silver and copper, as well as bronze paw feet, lion's head medallion bolts and leather strap seats, the latter usually augmented with a cushion. Equally prestigious, Roman thrones of marble, limestone or wood were a direct development of the earlier Greek models, although those raised on legs, rather than with solid sides, tended to be larger and heavier than their predecessors.

The Roman equivalent of the Greek *klismos* was the *cathedra*. Although it had a curved back its legs were straight, which gave it a more robust but decidedly less graceful appearance. Despite sometimes doubling up as a litter, it was far less prevalent and less inspirational to posterity.

By contrast, one of the most popular forms of Roman seating, the *lectus*, was to prove a prototype for variations of the chaise longue centuries later. Essentially a form of couch, the *lectus* was used extensively by the Romans, for formal and informal dining and drinking, at meetings and for informal conversation, and for generally relaxing. Most were raised on turned legs, and some had headboards and/or footboards (some had neither). Many were extravagantly embellished with metal mounts and inlaid or painted decoration. Upholstery, in the form of loose cushions or bolsters, with loose covers (often animal skins), could be equally ostentatious.

The rich repertoire of imagery used to decorate both it and the other types of Roman seating also became the basis for Classical and Neo-Classical decoration centuries later. The Romans adapted, and added to, inherited Greek motifs for decoration in the form of acanthus leaves; stalks, festoons and strings of husks; volutes (scrolls) and *paterae* (round or oval dish forms, each decorated with a formalized flower or rosette); cornucopias (stylized animal horns overflowing with ears of wheat and fruit); and shields, spears, arrows and other military trophies. Significant revivals of all these Roman motifs began during the European Renaissance and recurred at regular intervals from then on – but especially on the French Empire, English Regency and American Federal chairs of the early 19th century.

Above
Here augmented with cushions, the folding X-frame stool known as a *sella curulis* was used by Roman senators and magistrates.

The Middle Ages

When the Western Roman Empire finally succumbed to the Germanic tribes in 476CE, it saw the end of more than 600 years of Roman dominion. The dislocation and territorial disputes meant that the Classical styles favoured by Rome fell into decline; however, the Eastern Roman Empire, centred in Constantinople, was still under the influence of Rome through an increasingly powerful papacy. Classical Roman forms remained, but were influenced strongly by the East, with formal abstract ornamentation. The move away from Classical reserve, and a delight in colourful ornamentation, was to typify the Middle Ages.

The most common pieces of furniture, as evidenced in manuscripts and mosaics, were chairs and thrones. Byzantine chairs were often based on the Egyptian X-frame, with a leather seat and terminals elaborately carved with beasts' heads, while at the lower end terminating in claws. They are often depicted in metal, but highly decorated wooden examples were also found. Chairs remained symbols of power, and size was paramount. Painted benches, with turned feet, and X-frame stools were found in aristocratic homes.

In Western Europe the Barbaric invasions had effectively swept away many of the skills of the cabinet-maker, apart from at palaces and monasteries. The chair 'design' went back to primitive methods of construction – hewing out logs or branches with sharpened ends fixed into other members. As many of the nobles were peripatetic, travelling long distances between grand estates, chairs had to be easily transportable.

As the centuries passed, however, chair-making skills again improved, and in the Romanesque period (the 11th and 12th centuries) many architecturally decorated throne-like chairs had turned members and were painted in bright colours and gilded. The chair was essentially ceremonial, with high backs with uprights ending in finials. Formal and in some ways sedate, the Romanesque style gradually gave way to the soaring architecture of the Gothic vocabulary of ornament – the rounded arch giving way to the pointed. Gothic was a Norman innovation fusing Burgundian traditions with Islamic elements from conquered Sicily, where the pointed arch, a relic of Saracen invasion, was discovered. The ecclesiastical ornament of the great cathedrals of northern Europe formed the basis of Gothic furniture design: the Coronation Chair in London's Westminster Abbey is a famous example of high-status furniture at its most architectural and most decorative, with bright paintwork and gilding.

The Renaissance

The Renaissance, meaning 'rebirth', was a cultural movement that spanned roughly the 14th to the 17th centuries, beginning in Italy in the late Middle Ages and gradually spreading around Europe. In the 14th century the Italian cities of Florence, Venice, Rome and Milan emerged from a period of civil strife into a new age of prosperity. The republican attitudes of Florence in particular predisposed students at the universities to reappraise the design, philosophy, science and art of ancient Rome and Greece.

The cities were awash with artists seeking commissions from rich merchants. The *palazzi* were opulently decorated – walls were all-over frescoed, ceilings were carved and gilded, and furniture was decorated with marquetry and inlays of ivory and precious woods. Paintings of the period, however, show that, to the modern eye, these sumptuous houses were sparsely furnished. With the spread of the mood of civic humanism that informed the Renaissance mind, chairs – which had always been a symbol of power – were made more accessible to all, and the X-frame chair with leather seat became as popular in Renaissance Italy as it had been in antiquity.

In France the Renaissance ideals arrived before the beginning of the 16th century. By the end of that century, oak had been gradually replaced by walnut, and the imposing throne chair of the Gothic period gave way to a lighter chair with a low back and open arms, often carved with ram's head terminals. The *chaise caquetoire* (loosely translated as 'gossiping chair'), or *chaise à femme*, had a tall and narrow back, a wide trapezoidal seat and bowed arms to deal with the ladies' wide skirts. There was also more interest in comfort, with many chairs having padded backs and seats covered in rich silks and wools, often with fringes.

In England the homes of the Tudor nobles were centred on the great hall, as they had been in the Middle Ages, although increasingly families also had private rooms. Furniture remained the domain of the joiner, who carried on creating extremely functional oak furniture along traditional lines until the second half of the 17th century. In the 16th century the main chair in the great hall was a joined chair with framed and panelled back, sides and seat. Decoration was traditional, but often influenced by imported craftsmen and furniture from Italy. Pseudo-Classical motifs were found intertwined with Tudor roses and Gothic tracery. By the early 17th century the joined chair had become lighter, having shed the panels beneath the seat and arms, which were now scrolled. Turned decoration (shaped on a lathe) appeared in open-frame English joinery around the middle of the 16th century, and after this date most chairs had turned legs.

China

Archaeological excavations have revealed that wooden furniture had been made in China for hundreds of years BCE; however, the types of wooden seating that were to influence the design in the Western world emerged during the Tang and Song dynasties, c.618–1279CE. Moreover, they were fully developed only during the Ming Dynasty of 1368–1644CE, and the first hundred years or so of the Qing Dynasty that immediately followed – a period in which increased trade with the West fuelled prosperity and greater demand for high-quality furniture.

This is not to say, however, that chairs were in widespread use in China. The traditional practice of eating and drinking at low tables meant that cushions, low benches and, as had been the case in Egypt, Greece and Rome, stools (including folding versions) were the most common forms of seating. By contrast, chairs, without or without arms, were a symbol of power and were restricted to dignitaries, heads of households and esteemed scholars.

The wooden 'yokeback' was the earliest and most prevalent of these chairs. So-called because the horizontal rail above the central back-splat undulated like the yoke used to harness oxen, it could be an armchair or armless. Subsequent developments included round and U- or horseshoe-shaped top rails, and also cross-legged folding versions. Some of the latter, which were developed from an ancient folding stool known as a *hu-ch'uang*, featured sloping backs that encouraged a partly reclined or slumped posture, and hence were referred to as 'drunken lords'. Many of these chairs incorporated a front stretcher, which served as a supportive brace and a footrest – a feature also often found on *meiguiyi* armchairs, which had low rectangular backs and sides of carved latticework or fretwork.

Opposite
Carved from wood, painted and gilded, and enclosing the Stone of Scone, the Coronation Chair in London's Westminster Abbey was commissioned c.1300 by Edward I.

Above right
Both the joined armchair, or wainscot (front left), and the *chaise caquetoire*, or gossiping chair (back right), were made from solid oak in the 17th century.

While many vernacular, workaday chairs were constructed from inexpensive bamboo, the best chairs were made from indigenous hardwoods, notably *huanghuali* (a yellowish rosewood) and *zitan* (a variety of sandalwood). Sophisticated construction techniques included mitred and mortise-and-tenon joints and, whenever possible, cutting even large curved components from single pieces of timber to make them smooth and seamless. Decoration, other than open or relief carving (which became more extensive after the Ming period), was usually confined to the natural colour, figuring and grain of the wood. Nevertheless, coloured lacquer-work finishes were sometimes applied and did provide greater resistance to insect infestation. It was, however, the aesthetic qualities of these chairs – their clarity of form and graceful lines – that were to endear them to Western designers from the 17th century onwards.

The 17th Century: Baroque

The 17th century was a period of unbridled wealth and empire building. In Italy the papacy reasserted its dominance, and successive popes commissioned architects to build impressive buildings and monuments in Rome. The exuberant theatrical sculptural style that it spawned, which was intended to show the wealth and power of the Catholic Church, became known as Baroque.

Influenced by Baroque architecture and sculpture, the furniture commissioned for the staterooms in the grand palaces was designed on a suitably grand scale, and many of its creators were sculptors rather than cabinet-makers. The main decorative themes were based on Classical and Renaissance motifs, and the style relied on fanciful decoration and precious materials. Chairs were embellished with marquetry and elaborate carving, with intricately pierced splats, and were often gilded.

Increased trade with the Far East provided furniture-makers with a wealth of exotic materials, including rosewood and ebony, tortoiseshell, mother-of pearl and semiprecious stones. As the century progressed, more furniture was imported from the Far East and the cabinet-makers were influenced by lacquer work from China and Japan, and caned furniture from India. High-backed chairs were often upholstered for greater comfort, but only for the wealthiest nobility. Silks and velvets from Italy were extremely expensive, and to have an elaborately upholstered chair was a powerful status symbol.

In England during the reign of Charles I (from 1625–49), many craftsmen from the Low Countries, France and Italy came to work in the palaces and grand houses. They brought with them high-status styles and designs, although the English Baroque remained more restrained than Italian. This taste for the most fashionable styles from mainland Europe was reinforced with the Restoration in 1660, when the monarchy was re-established and Charles II was crowned King. Walnut became the most popular wood, and caned chairs with twist-turned frames graced the palaces and country seats of the aristocracy.

Cabinet-makers and joiners from the Low Countries came to England with the accession of William III and Mary in 1689, in particular the French Huguenot architect and furniture designer Daniel Marot (1661–1752).

American furniture of the period was based on English Jacobean models. Most chairs produced were of the 'stick' variety and were a simpler version of the English 'thrown' chair, with the chair made completely of turned members, sometimes with finely turned finials.

Top left
Called a 'horseshoe chair' after the shape of its one-piece back rail and arms, this example was made from *huanghuali* wood c.1550–1650 during the Ming Dynasty.

Bottom left
The Doge of Venice's magnificent upholstered giltwood throne is carved in the ornate Baroque style and resides at the city's Church of Xan Zanipolo.

In the early years of the 17th century, Henry IV of France encouraged foreign craftsmen, mainly from the Low Countries and Italy, to work as cabinet-makers. Furniture became ever more opulent during the regency of Maria de' Medici and the reign of Louis XIII. Chairs, often made of walnut, were becoming more comfortable with lavish upholstery. The seats were wider and backs higher, and chair legs were often turned or elaborately carved. The wing chair was introduced in the middle of the century.

In 1661 Louis XIV, the Sun King, took control in France, and a new age of opulence began. The following year he gathered together some of the finest craftsmen and installed them in the Gobelins workshops to produce tapestries and other sumptuous furnishings for the royal palaces. Motifs included flora and fauna, grotesques and arabesques. The *fauteuil*, an armchair with a much lighter wooden frame, often gilded, had open arms and an upholstered seat and back, and the crest, arms and legs of the chairs were exquisitely carved. In 1682 Louis moved the court to the Palace of Versailles, where many of the rooms were designed by Charles Le Brun (1619–90). Much of the furnishing incorporated motifs associated with the Sun King, such as interlaced letter Ls, the fleur-de-lys and the sunburst. The most celebrated furniture-maker of the Louis XIV period was André-Charles Boulle (1642–1732), whose monumental furniture was inlaid with elaborate tortoiseshell and brass marquetry.

The Early to Mid-18th Century: Régence and Rococo

In the first half of the 18th century, the influence of Italy, Spain and the Low Countries began to decrease gradually. Across Europe there was the rise of a wealthy middle class, especially after the end of the War of Spanish Succession in 1713, which heralded a period of peace and growing prosperity.

In the early years of the century, furniture design was mainly influenced by France, where the lighter style reflected the pleasure in entertaining and convivial pursuits. When Louis XIV died in 1715, Philippe, Duke of Orléans, was made Regent for the young King Louis XV, and the period from 1715–23 is known as the Régence. The Duke of Orléans moved the court back to the Palais Royal in Paris. The Italian-trained architect Gilles-Marie Oppenord (1672–1742) remodelled the Palais Royal and created a more fluid, sensual asymmetrical, curvilinear style with naturalistic flowers and mythical figures, which foreshadowed the spirit of Rococo.

The most important stylistic effect on the chair was that the legs, instead of being straight, became slightly curved while, in the main, retaining the cross-stretcher. Another pivotal design change was instigated by developments in women's fashion. The popularity of the hooped skirt, from about 1720, required that chair seats be widened and the arms shortened. In addition, the remarkable hairstyles of the day dictated that chair backs be lowered. The *fauteuil*, with its open sides, and the more enclosed tub-like *bergère* were often upholstered in rich silks to mirror the drapes in the salon. Chairs were no longer all placed against the panelled walls, but could be put in the centre of the room to facilitate conversation.

The style that had its infancy during the Régence came to fruition under Louis XV. Rococo was the antithesis of Classical severity. Deriving its name from the shellwork and rockwork, or rocaille, found in the garden grottoes of the period, Rococo incorporated Renaissance and Baroque motifs, such as shells and masks, in abundance, but with a more delicate touch than

Bottom right
Made c.1750, this painted and giltwood French *fauteuil* displays, in its cabriole legs, serpentine seat rails, curved back and arm supports, the elegant curves of the Rococo style.

Top right
A Dutch armchair with cabriole legs, ball-and-claw feet, a baluster back-splat, shepherd's crook arms, and floral marquetry, made c.1840 in the English George II style.

previously, and usually in an asymmetrical arrangement. The effect was frivolous and feminine, embracing C- and S-scrolls, scallop shells, flowers, cupids and arabesques. One of the high points of the style was the work of the designer Juste-Aurèle Meissonier (1695–1750), who decorated the bedchamber of Louis XV with mythical beasts, asymmetrical waterfalls, shells and icicles.

The fashion for textiles and decorative objects imported from the Far East, which had developed in the previous century, reached a peak during the Rococo era, and chinoiserie (European versions of Eastern motifs) also became popular. The 'dreams of China' were not new, but the portrayal was more romantic than in the 17th century. Dragons and other Oriental beasts lent their sinuous shapes to Rococo ornament.

There was a general demand for more comfortable living. New rooms appeared – salons both large and small where people could converse, play games and listen to music. The influence of the Marquise de Pompadour, mistress of Louis XV, was indicative of the increasing social importance of women. This led to the development of small salon chairs that were lighter and more curvaceous, many with the new cabriole leg, which was a dramatic break with earlier styles. The cabriole was based on the hind leg of an animal and came from Chinese designs, as did that favoured terminus of the cabriole leg, the ball-and-claw foot, which derives from the Chinese motif of the dragon's claw clutching the pearl of wisdom. On important pieces, cabriole legs also often had highly decorated 'knees'.

Britain at this time was building its Empire. During the Queen Anne period, 1702–14 (although the style outlived the monarch), a Dutch-style chair with a solid vase-shaped back-splat, cabriole legs and pad feet became synonymous with the period. Chairs from the Queen Anne and George I (1714–27) periods are often in walnut or walnut-veneered oak. As a result of the war with France, British furniture-makers, as well as architects, looked beyond France for inspiration, back to the drawings of the Italian architect Andrea Palladio (1508–80). This Palladian revival was popular with the educated and well-travelled nobility from the 1720s to the 1740s. The cornerstone of the style was Classical symmetry.

By the early 18th century many British craftsmen were working on the east coast of the American colonies. This was a period of rapid economic growth for the colonies, with the emergence of a wealthy merchant class who built impressive homes and furnished them accordingly. The most significant innovation was the introduction of the cabriole leg on the Queen Anne chair; based on the English example, it remained popular from 1720–50 and gave dramatic fluidity to the style. The chairs tended to have balloon-shaped seats and solid vase-shaped splats. The crest rails were often decorated with carved shells.

The Mid- to Late 18th Century: Neo-Classicism

The second half of the 18th century saw a renewed interest in and knowledge of Classical architecture and design. This had begun with the excavations at the buried Roman towns of Herculaneum and Pompeii, from 1738, and had been further encouraged by the publication in 1762 of *Antiquities of Athens* by James Stuart and Nicholas Revett. Aristocratic travellers, including architects and designers on the 'Grand Tour', increased awareness of the Classical world. Initially this meant that Classical motifs were once again applied to furniture and that symmetry was re-introduced. But with philosophers, artists and writers looking back to the

Above left
Selectively painted, this American 'bow-back' Windsor armchair from the second half of the 18th century features bamboo-turned legs, H-stretcher and arm supports.

ideals and practices of the Classical world, the Neo-Classical movement had a far-reaching effect on all elements of architecture and interior design. Alongside this, the introduction of the steam engine in the 1770s to drive machinery meant that textiles and eventually furniture could be produced in much larger quantities.

France was again the style leader in this reappraisal of Classical style, although Rococo was still influential well into the 1770s. The period 1760–75 is known as Transitional, as it displays elements of both Rococo and Neo-Classical. A reaction to the excesses of Rococo caused the engraver Nicolas Cochin in 1754 to entreat his fellow Frenchmen to return to the 'way of good taste of the preceding century'. Again the published word was a catalyst. The Comte de Caylus published between 1752 and 1767 the seven volumes of his *Recueil d'antiquités égyptiennes, étrusques, grecques, romaines et gauloises* ('Collection of Egyptian, Etruscan, Greek, Roman and Gallic Antiquities'), in which he illustrated the styles of the ancient world. The effect on the fashionable classes in France was such that in 1763 Baron Grimm declared that *'tout à Paris est à la grecque'* ('everything in Paris is in the Greek style'). By the time Louis XVI succeeded to the throne in 1774, the Neo-Classical style was well established.

At the heart of the distinction between Rococo and Neo-Classical is the replacement of the curvaceous with the rectilinear, and of asymmetry with symmetry. Chair backs became rectangular, oval or shield-shaped, and legs were usually turned and reeded or fluted, with reference to Classical architectural columns. The frames of the chairs were often gilded and carved with Classical motifs such as acanthus and anthemion. In the 1780s *ébénistes* such as Georges Jacob (1739–1814) pierced splats with motifs including lyres and wheat sheaves, often flanked by reeded columns. The lack of the sensuous curves of the Rococo in the chairs of Louis XVI did not, however, result in a severe style. Indeed the richly upholstered medallion-shaped back with elliptical top rail, rounded front seat rail and armrests that curve from the back rail of the Louis XVI chair created a highly opulent style.

The start of the French Revolution in 1789 brought an end to the furniture-makers' guild system and, as a large number of the aristocratic patrons fell victim to the guillotine or fled France, the quality of French furniture also diminished. The simpler Etruscan decorative style found favour during the Directoire and Consulate periods that followed (1795–1804). Notably, mahogany chairs inspired by English examples proved popular.

Swedish monarchs had long looked to France for design inspiration. The flowering of the Swedish Neo-Classical style, termed Gustavian after King Gustav III, who reigned from 1771–92, refers to the period from 1760 to 1810. Gustav had spent time at Versailles and wanted to emulate the French Neo-Classical style in his palaces. The chairs produced in Sweden are more rectilinear than the French and tend to be painted rather than gilded.

In England the accession of George III to the throne in 1760 heralded a golden period for English furniture design. One of the most influential figures was the Scottish architect Robert Adam (1728–92), who had spent nearly five years on a Grand Tour and studying in Italy. He was greatly influenced by Roman antiquity, and his drawings of festoons of husks or bellflowers, *paterae*, Vitruvian scrolls, anthemia, urns, oval medallions and tripods would later be reflected in his interiors. Adam mainly designed interiors and commissioned furniture to be made by other luminaries of the period, including Thomas Chippendale and John Linnell. Initially, in the early

Bottom right
The rectilinear qualities of French Neo-Classical taste are evident in this late-18th-century painted and gilded Swedish Gustavian-style armchair.

Top right
Made in Philadelphia, this Marie Antoinette suite armchair is fashioned in the French Louis XVI Neo-Classical style of the late 18th century.

1760s, Adam's motifs of Classical sphinxes and delicate formalized scrolls of foliage were applied to essentially Rococo chairs with cabriole legs; however, he rapidly moved to furniture designed in the Classical taste, with straight tapering square-section legs.

In 1754 Thomas Chippendale (c.1718–79) published *The Gentleman and Cabinet-Maker's Director*, which revolutionized the way in which furniture styles were disseminated. The book was the first pattern book to concentrate only on furniture and gave examples of all the prevailing styles: French, Gothic, Chinese and Rococo. The French *fauteuil*, with its scrolling arms, rails and legs, adapted particularly well to the Neo-Classical style. Forms became lighter with straight square legs, which by the 1780s had become more tapered.

Such was the demand for more furniture in the 'new' style in England and America that George Hepplewhite's widow published *The Cabinet-Maker and Upholsterer's Guide* in 1788, two years after his death. Hepplewhite (c.1727–86) is remembered in particular for his graceful and elegant chairs with their distinctive shield-, oval- or heart-shaped backs. He was a great advocate of Adam style, which can be seen in the back-splats shaped like vases or urns with festoons of drapery, rosettes, ears of wheat or Prince of Wales's feathers, either carved or painted. The legs were typically straight and tapering, although on occasion a slender baluster was used.

The next pattern book to be published to great acclaim was by Thomas Sheraton (1751–1806); *The Cabinet-Maker and Upholsterer's Drawing-Book* was first issued in 1791–3. Sheraton's chairs were almost all of square-back design and, although he embraced the vase, urn, leaf and drapery motifs, they had a strong vertical emphasis.

These pattern books also had a great impact on the furniture styles in the American colonies. As previously there was, however, a time-lag. The style that superseded American Queen Anne in the early 1760s is rather loosely described as American Chippendale, and being essentially inspired by the latter's pattern books it meant that the Rococo style and especially elements of the style, were still in-vogue in America after they had fallen out of fashion in Europe. The chairs made – notably in Philadelphia, a leading centre of production – were of generous proportions, with a broad plain splat, scroll cresting, and typically a carved shell on the centre of the seat frame and trifid feet. Although rather conservative, this style was transformed when the splat was pierced and carved with naturalistic ornament and the ball-and-claw foot was adopted. Some of the most sophisticated American chairs of the period have delicate Gothic tracery carving to the back-splat, and volute or scroll feet, while some of the increasingly popular upholstered armchairs have straight carved 'Marlborough' legs and block feet.

After the American War of Independence (1775–83), Chippendale-style chairs were still produced, but a new Federal style developed loosely based on the Neo-Classical designs of Hepplewhite and Sheraton. Early Federal chairs were refined and restrained, with simple geometric shapes and shield, oval or square backs. Legs were slender, tapered and square, or slightly vase-shaped and reeded. Feet were usually arrow- or spade-shaped. Many chairs had painted finishes displaying Classical motifs, such as *paterae*, bellflowers and vases of flowers. The proud emblem of the new American republic, the bald eagle, also became a popular motif. As to upholstery, imported silks, often with a striped pattern, were employed for the finest chairs, while cotton- or wool-woven fabrics were used on lesser chairs.

Above
Despite the emergence of Neo-Classicism, Chippendale Rococo-design chairs, such as this superb example from Philadelphia, continued to be made in America in the late 18th century.

The Early 19th Century: A New Classicism

France had declared war on the rest of Europe in 1792 and set about creating republics based on the French model, until its defeat in 1815. Napoleon Bonaparte became First Consul in 1799 and declared himself Emperor in 1804. The Empire style, named after the Napoleonic Empire of this period, was a more austere Classical style than the pre-Revolutionary version, which was now considered too ostentatious.

Two conquests in 1797 had a great influence on the designs of furniture: the French won the Battle of the Pyramids in Egypt, and Napoleon's army captured Rome. Napoleon was obsessed with the power and grandeur of Imperial Rome and ancient Egypt. His Egyptian campaign led to associated motifs (collectively known as Egyptiennerie), including sphinx heads, scarabs, crocodile motifs and palmettes, being central to the French Empire style.

The dissemination of the style was accelerated by Napoleon's relatives who ruled the countries he had conquered: Germany, Italy, the Netherlands and Spain. So powerful was the impact of the style that even countries hostile to Napoleon, such as Russia and to a certain extent Britain, were influenced. Chairs became dramatic statements – there were bold rectilinear or overscrolled backs, with upholstered panels showing architectural affinities; the arms could be supported by human or swan forms (the latter being Empress Josephine's favoured motif). The back legs were often of Grecian sabre shape, and the front legs were frequently turned, in spindle, column or baluster forms. Many fabrics were striped in blue, red, yellow or green, and many had motifs associated with Napoleon, such as the omnipresent bee, the Roman Imperial eagle and the gilt N within laurels. Chairs were much influenced by the designs of the ancient world, notably the *klismos* chair.

Although the Regency period in Britain, during which the Prince of Wales acted as Regent for his father, George III, was from 1811–20, the Regency style-period runs from the late 1790s to the 1830s. British furniture in the early 19th century was simple and elegant. Two of the main types of chair were the *klismos* and the *currule*. The sphinx became one of the most popular motifs. The backs of chairs gradually adopted a horizontal instead of a vertical emphasis, while the arms began to be shaped in a downward-curving scroll.

Painted chair backs with Classical motifs were once more in great demand. One of the most identifiable pieces of Regency furniture is the Trafalgar chair of 1805, named after Nelson's naval victory; the distinctive back rail had cable or rope moulding. Chair backs were at times inlaid in brass, reminiscent of the boulle work on Louis XIV chairs.

There was a feeling that the style should return to the 'pure spirit of antiquity', as exemplified in Thomas Hope's *Household Furniture and Interior Decoration*, published in 1807. This showed the interiors of his house on Duchess Street, London. Hope (1769–1831) designed much of the furniture himself in the precise forms of Roman, Greek and Egyptian decorative vocabulary.

As well as marking a return to a more authentic Classical style, this was an opulent period with a taste for the exotic, led by the Prince Regent himself. Chinoiserie became extremely popular, particularly following the completion of the 'Chinese' rooms in Brighton's Royal Pavilion for the Prince Regent, shortly after he became George IV. Chairs were japanned black and red, or black and gold, to emulate lacquer, or were made from bamboo or turned and painted to simulate bamboo.

Top
Designed c. 1808 by Benjamin Latrobe, this American side chair is a re-interpretation of the Greek *klismos* chair from Classical antiquity.

Above
An early 19th-century mahogany and ormolu-mounted Russian armchair fashioned in the Empire style with ancient Egyptian imagery.

Biedermeier furniture, which was popular from the 1800s to the 1850s, was a much simpler interpretation of Classicism than the Empire style and was much favoured by the middle classes of Germany, Austria and Scandinavia. It was made from local woods such as pear, birch, walnut and cherry, combined with dark elm and thuya wood. The chairs were essentially rectilinear with no carving, the only decoration being Classical motifs in the contrasting pale and dark woods.

In the United States, the early Federal period's Neo-Classicism based on Adam, Hepplewhite and Sheraton had produced a wonderfully light, delicate style. In the later Federal period the style became heavier, and chairs were often based on the *klismos* chair. The best-quality chairs were designed by highly skilled craftsmen such as Duncan Phyfe (1768–1854). His chairs typically had harp, urn or lyre backs, sabre legs with paw feet and classical decoration of swags, wheat sheaves and cornucopia. American Empire furniture became fashionable around 1815. This style was inspired by the delicate early Federal style, but the chairs were bulkier and more ornate, with sabre or *currule* legs terminating in carved animal or large ball feet. The splats were large vase-shaped splats or *demi-lune* splats flanked by reeded stiles with a curved and rolled top rail.

The Mid- to Late 19th Century: Battle of the Styles

By the middle of the 19th century, as the furniture-makers and their patrons – often now the nouveau riche middle class – looked back at the great wealth of historical styles, the age of the revival dawned. From the frivolous Rococo emanating from France to the more sober Gothic popular in Britain, nations everywhere looked to the past. These revivals were happily combined in interiors and even in individual pieces of furniture: Renaissance, Elizabethan (merging with Tudor, Jacobean and Stuart), Classical (with an emphasis on Greek), Rococo (taken from the grand designs of Louis XV) and Gothic elements vied for supremacy. In the hands of a great designer this eclecticism could work, but too often it created ungainly pieces.

Increasing industrialization allowed furniture to be made more quickly and cheaply. Veneers could be cut to the same thinness, and carving took a fraction of the time of hand carving – but quality was sacrificed. Furniture design, once a respected craft, was now an industrial process. Design was a victim of the machine. Size and overblown decoration took over from taste and proportion. Forms such as the balloon-back chair with a pierced scroll splat and cabriole legs suited the Victorian parlour and dining room.

Other notable developments included the fashion for overstuffed seats and deeply padded chair backs. This was not only made possible, but also substantially fuelled by the introduction of coiled springs, which required a thick layer of padding to prevent them from piercing expensive top covers, and also promoted the fashion for buttoning – deep-set buttons being required to hold the padding and springs in position. At the same time, increasing imports from India, China and Japan inspired European furniture-makers to employ diverse Oriental and Asian motifs, which added to the decorative exoticism of many late 19th-century interiors. Innovative designers of the period included Michael Thonet (1796–1871), who perfected a process for steam-bending laminate veneers in his factory in Boppard am Rhein, now part of Germany. This allowed him to produce some of the most successful chairs of the 19th century and paved the way for the designs of Charles and Ray Eames a century later.

Above
Gebrüder Thonet began making its revolutionary steamed and press-moulded bentwood chairs in the early 1850s. Its classic bentwood rocker dates from c.1880.

Top
Made in one of North America's Shaker communities, these 19th-century ladderbacks have suitably plain lunette-shaped back slats and appropriately rustic rush seats.

The Late 19th Century: The Arts and Crafts Movement

As early as the 1860s, a rejection of the historicism and stylistic eclecticism of Victorian furniture emerged in Britain under the banner of the Arts and Crafts movement. Its members were critical of both the poor quality and the over-ornamentation of mass-produced Victorian furnishings. The movement was also fuelled by the belief that the decoration of all artefacts should be an integral part of their design. To most British Arts and Crafts designers this meant a revival of the pre-industrial standards of craftsmanship that had been established during the Middle Ages and was still practised in many rural areas. It also meant the use of 'honest', unpretentious forms of decoration.

On many Arts and Crafts chairs, the decoration was confined to the nature of the construction – mortise-and-through-tenon joints were a recurring feature – and the natural figuring and grain of the wood (especially if it was oak). Additional decoration, when employed, was largely derived from the medieval English and secularized Gothic vocabularies of ornament, mostly in the form of carved or pierced motifs depicting flora and fauna.

In Britain one of the founders of the movement, and its leading light, was William Morris (1834–96). The most popular design sold by his company, Morris & Co., was the ash-framed Sussex chair. Based on a traditional turned country chair, it had spindles in the back and a hand-woven rush seat. Also well received, and very influential in the United States, was the company's Morris chair – a large, box-like armchair with an ebonized frame and an adjustable back. William Morris's influence endured in areas such as the Cotswolds later in the century with craftsmen including Ernest William Gimson, Sidney and Ernest Barnsley and Robert 'Mouseman' Thompson.

In the United States the Arts and Crafts ethos flowered from the late 1890s to the early 1920s as the Craftsman movement. Gustav Stickley (1858–1942) and his four brothers were at the forefront. After visiting Europe, Stickley set up a company in 1898 in Eastwood, New York, producing furniture inspired by William Morris, although some spindle-backs were influenced by the leading American architect Frank Lloyd Wright. The *Craftsman* magazine, launched by Stickley in 1901, was crucial in disseminating the style throughout the United States.

By this time Grand Rapids, Michigan, had became a major centre for the manufacture of high-quality furniture. There, the craftsman-designer Charles Limbert (1854–1923) produced what he described as Dutch Arts and Crafts chairs. His company was particularly well known for its chairs in geometric forms with heart-shaped cutouts. In California, the architects Greene and Greene also embraced the Arts and Crafts style, designing bungalows and creating fine bespoke furniture, with a strong horizontal line to their chairs.

Turn of the Century: Art Nouveau

The same impetus that gave rise to the Arts and Crafts movement in Britain and the United States – the rejection of the poor-quality, mass-produced furnishings of the industrialized age – gave birth in Europe to the Art Nouveau movement. Taking its name from the Parisian shop of Siegfried Bing, L'Art nouveau, which opened in 1895, the style was obvious on the streets of Europe: on the buildings, the posters, the Paris Metro signs. An integrated style, it also pervaded the interiors, furnishings, glass, sculpture and even jewellery. French Art Nouveau was

Top
With its cabriole legs, scrolled arm supports, serpentine back, and plump button-backed upholstery, this armchair is fashioned in the Victorian Rococo-revival style.

Above
Manufactured c.1870 by Morris & Co., the rush-seated spindle-back 'Sussex' chair exemplified the Arts and Crafts Movement revival of traditional rustic chair-making.

showcased at the Exposition Universelle in Paris in 1900, with various pavilions, including Bing's, displaying high-quality Art Nouveau at its most unified.

In France and Belgium the style was flowing and curvilinear, and strongly influenced by nature, particularly the sinuous curves of flora and fauna and the sensuous female form. The *ébénistes* in the Paris School looked back to the high-quality Rococo work produced during the reign of Louis XV. The most dominant decorative features to influence furniture design were organic scrolling shapes, whiplash curves and asymmetry. While inspired by nature, the designers used a formalized, stylized repertoire. Many chairs were carved in walnut with floral and foliate motifs. The upholstery could be leather, embossed with sinuous floral imagery, or similarly patterned cottons or silks. The feet were often carved, and outsplayed or flared.

The School of Nancy, an Art Nouveau movement based in the city of Nancy, produced exuberant, fluid curvilinear chairs inspired by nature, while retaining more overall symmetry. Many of the movement's chairs, such as those by Louis Majorelle (1859–1926), have wide splats to display floral marquetry designs created in exotic timbers.

The Belgian style was similar to the French, again relying on a large vocabulary of natural motifs and organic forms, while Italy and Spain created the most exotic Art Nouveau chairs. Many exhibited the new style with elaborately carved back-splats with natural forms, while retaining restrained, undecorated curves on stiles and legs. In every style there is a maverick, a one-off, and such was the Italian designer Carlo Bugatti (1856–1940). His fantasy style was influenced by nature, but even more by Moorish, Egyptian and Japanese art. In Spain, the architect Antoni Gaudí (1852–1926) created wonderfully sensuous chairs with organic curves and plant and flower motifs.

In Scotland, Austria and Germany a more rectilinear style emerged. Charles Rennie Mackintosh, the leader of the Glasgow School (a group of architects and designers associated with the Glasgow School of Art), designed high-backed chairs that were either oak or beech with cut out geometric shapes or were painted off-white or pastel shades with stylized roses. Although Mackintosh's style was not regarded highly in the rest of Britain, where a diluted French style proliferated, he was extremely influential in Austria and Germany, particularly after he exhibited at the eighth Secession exhibition in Vienna in 1900. In Austria some designers embraced the floral embodiment of Art Nouveau, but most were influenced by the Secession as well as the Glasgow School. Jugendstil, the German version of Art Nouveau, showed the influence of natural forms and favoured rectilinear shapes and restrained curves.

The Early 20th Century: Art Deco

The Art Deco style, which flourished after World War I, was an amalgam of many different styles and movements of the early 20th century, including Constructivism, Cubism, Modernism, Classicism, Exoticism and Futurism. Its popularity peaked in Europe during the Roaring Twenties, with its 'high' feminine French style, and continued strongly in the United States through the 1930s, with its more masculine streamlined geometric and skyscraper styles. While designers had always been very influential in establishing furniture styles in the past, from the 1920s onwards they became not only pivotal to changing aesthetics, but style brands in their own right as well.

The French style, which harked back to the high-quality *ébénistes* of the 18th century, was completely at odds with the industrial design of the United States, Germany and Britain. The

Top left
Typified by this side chair of c.1900, Carlo Bugatti's unique interpretation of Art Nouveau was inspired by a fusion of Egyptian, Byzantine, Moorish and Japanese forms and imagery.

Bottom left
Characteristic Art Nouveau motifs carved in this Italian side chair of c.1900 include 'femme fleurs', and flora and fauna – notably asymmetrical whiplash foliate forms.

French designer saw France as the world style leader and relied on the wealthy patron rather than the mass market. French Art Deco was showcased at the 1925 Paris Exposition Internationale des Arts Décoratifs et Industriels Modernes, from which Art Deco derived its name. This was French design at its most elite, with high-quality woods and carving. Veneers of many exotic woods with distinctive grains, such as ebony and sycamore, were used, as were shagreen, lacquer and ivory. Chairs had curved undulating wooden frames that recalled the 18th-century *bergères*. Splats made from rich timbers were decorated with stylized motifs, geometric patterns, foliage, fountains or fruit. Designers such as Émile-Jacques Ruhlmann (1879–1933) used veneers of macasser ebony, palisander, burr amboyna and amaranth. Many Art Deco chairs were made of luxurious timber, with shaped backs and slender tapered legs, the latter often terminating in sabots of ivory or bronze.

Some American designers, such as Eugene Schoen, did expensive handcrafted work in the style of the French, but most were intent on producing high-style pieces that could be mass-produced. Designers such as Paul Frankl, Donald Deskey and Kem Weber were influenced by Bauhaus design. They combined exotic timbers with new materials such as aluminium, steel, polished steel and Bakelite. American designers were obsessed with the machine age, and by the 1930s chairs were being made in the new materials of tubular steel, vinyl and chromed metal, many with geometric lines.

The Early 20th Century: Modernism

World War I and the associated horrors and devastation of homes and lives had an indelible effect on architects and designers. In the aftermath of the war, superfluous decoration was abandoned in favour of severe lines; functionalism was seen as superior to delight. There was also a rejection of the past as inspiration for designs. With new technology and materials, designers sought to forge a future in which the new, industrialized furniture-production process would be lauded for its honesty, integrity and streamlined simplicity. Many furniture designers were also aware of the need to produce inexpensive furniture for the masses.

Bending tubular steel, sometimes chrome-plated, and plywood allowed designers to create flowing, curvaceous lines, while the rejection of surface decoration led designers to revere the exposed structure of the piece. The zenith for the Modernist chair designer was the cantilever, which did away with the notion that a chair had to have four legs, while imbuing it with graceful, sinuous curves. Many Modernist designers embodied Henry Ford's mantra of 'any colour so long as it's black', as they felt that colour often detracted from the inherent beauty of the structure of the chair.

The nation most dedicated to the 'new design' was Germany. The Deutscher Werkbund (German Work Foundation), founded in Munich in 1907, had already explored the relationship between art and industry with such luminaries as Peter Behrens, Richard Riemerschmid and Josef Maria Olbrich. After World War I, the German designers were convinced that 'standardization' was the way forward. The Bauhaus, founded in 1919 by Walter Gropius in Weimar, was pivotal to the dissemination of the Modernist aesthetic. Gropius believed that the machine should be adopted by architects and designers, and this was enacted when the school moved to Dessau in 1924. Marcel Breuer (1902–81), a student turned tutor, was an innovator

Top right
Art Deco re-interpretation of a traditional French *bergère*, this luxurious c.1928 English armchair by Hille & Co. has leather-covered upholstery in a U-shaped walnut-veneered frame.

Bottom right
Designed c.1930 by Hans and Wassili Luckhardt, this German armchair is quintessential Modernism in its use of chromed tubular steel and a cantilevered construction.

in the use of tubular steel and leather-sling upholstery, culminating in the Wassily chair of 1925. A Werkbund exhibition in Stuttgart in 1927, entitled Die Wohnung (The Dwelling), brought both international acclaim and amazement. The 60 houses in the exhibition were designed by Walter Gropius, Le Corbusier, Mart Stam and others, and exhibited tubular-steel furniture to the public for the first time. The organizer of the exhibition, Ludwig Mies van der Rohe, despite being an advocate of functionalism, was keen that the resulting chairs should have a sympathetic human relationship.

In France, the *enfant terrible* of the conservative establishment was the Swiss-born architect and designer Charles-Édouard Jeanneret (1887–1965), called Le Corbusier, whose stark design rationale led to his pavilion at the 1925 Paris Exposition being compared to a prison cell. His famous battle cry 'The house is a machine for living in' was anathema to the art establishment, but many designers responded to this call to arms. Tubular steel was at the heart of the new style. Although initially expensive, it was lightweight, industrially manufactured and shockingly metallic.

Whether owing to the cold weather or to the craft tradition, the Scandinavians remained resolutely unimpressed by tubular steel. While favouring the minimalism of the German and some French designers, the Scandinavians developed a softer, more organic form of Modernism, dependent on the natural, undulating curves of bent plywood.

Mid-Century Modern

In furniture design, the recovery from World War II was led by the Americans and the Scandinavians. Many manufacturing techniques that had been introduced for the war effort were now made available to furniture designers, such as new ways of bonding wood. The ergonomically sensitive Scandinavian style promoted by Alvar Aalto became increasingly influential to post-war consumers. Scandinavian design remained true to its roots, literally, by honing the design of handcrafted wooden chairs. Imported teak became the wood of choice, as it was plentiful and cheap, and could be given a wonderful satin finish, well suited to the elegant organic lines of Scandinavian design. Function met form, met delight.

By the mid-1950s there was a more positive, even optimistic feeling in the air, and the sharp, stark lines of Modernism gave way to gentler curves and brighter colours. Many of the chair designers, such as Wendell Castle and Vladimir Kagan, produced sculptural, organic forms. Another trend that influenced the design of chairs was the idea of disposable furniture.

Owing to overproduction of oil, plastics became the furniture designers' plaything, particularly in the mid-1960s, while fibreglass and aluminium expanded the chair designers' repertoire. New plywood-moulding techniques and thinner steel rods allowed more organic and abstract designs. Charles and Ray Eames, with Eero Saarinen, were early pioneers of moulded plywood. The fact that it could be moulded in more than one direction gave designers the opportunity to experiment with compound curves. Stretch fabric, rubber and foam padding all allowed designers to create ever-more fabulous shapes that did not have to be controlled by the traditional structure of the chair.

Arne Jacobsen (1902–71) was regarded as the chair supremo of the mid-20th century. The Ant chair he designed in 1952 was the ideal chair for mass production, while his No.3107 chair, which appeared in 1955, is arguably the most popular chair ever designed. Jacobsen's later,

Top left
Designed c.1948 by Charles Eames, La Chaise is raised above a wooden base on iron rods. Its amoeba-like seat of moulded fibreglass is characteristic of mid-20th-century Organic Modernism.

Bottom left
Designed in 1965 by Olivier Mourgue, the Mid-Century Modern Djinn's polyurethane and metal frame is foam-padded and covered with a tight, swimming costume-like elasticated jersey fabric.

more organic chairs depended on a process of steam-moulding polystyrene beads, which under heat became foam, onto a fibreglass base.

One of the most influential design institutions in the mid-20th century was the Cranbrook Academy of Art in Michigan. Founded in 1932, it was the launching pad for a coterie of great designers including Charles and Ray Eames, Eero Saarinen, Harry Bertoia and Florence Knoll, who were inspired by the concept of marrying industry and art. Charles Eames (1907–78) and his wife Ray (1912–88) sought to experiment with inexpensive materials that could easily be mass-produced: plastic, fibreglass, moulded plywood and aluminium. In 1940, Charles Eames and his contemporary Eero Saarinen (1920–61) won the prestigious Organic Design in Home Furnishing competition, hosted by MoMA in New York, with moulded plywood designs.

American designers were testing the limits of old and new materials and were also using solid wood, laminated wood, fabric, tube and solid steel, and Perspex. The talented designer George Nelson, who, in 1946, became design director of the Herman Miller Furniture Co. of Michigan, ensured that this company was at the forefront of the new design movement. Another company to employ cutting-edge designers was Knoll International, which, mainly through the influence of Florence Knoll, produced designs by Isamu Noguchi and Harry Bertoia. Their designs were very sculptural and, for the conservative American consumer, quite daring.

Italy took a lead in this style-conscious era, and the industrial designers enjoying a boom in the 1950s added a touch of expressive elegance to Rationalist principles. The biomorphic designs of chairs of the period were often expressed in sensual, curvaceous lines. Designers such as Gio Ponti (1891–1971) were as much influenced by Italy's traditions of handcrafting and Classical vocabulary as the new machine age. Ponti never lost sight of the human proportions of the chair.

A Reductionist mania in the mid-20th century also led many designers to attempt to produce the perfect chair from one continuous piece of material. Verner Panton took this to its logical conclusion with the sinuous curves of his plywood S chair and his plastic Panton – both of which combined elegance, style, refinement and great strength.

Sheet metal, softened with brightly coloured upholstery, created some of the iconic chairs of the period, many of them displaying an almost organic abstraction. Tubular-metal chairs, by designers such as Harry Bertoia, also enjoyed a resurgence.

The 1950s and 1960s were the pinnacles of plastic. This material was everything the chair designers had dreamed of – adaptable, multipurpose, durable, waterproof, colourful and, most importantly, cheap. Injection-moulding technology allowed the designers to put into production some of their wildest fantasies, such as the Ball, the Pastil, the Egg and the Zocker – Pop Art furniture had arrived.

The Late 20th Century: Post-Modern and Contemporary

Post-Modernism marked the end of the designers' dream that it was possible to solve society's problems by using the machine and industrial technology. The oil-induced recession of the mid-1970s saw the utopian philosophies of the Modern movement treated with cynicism.

Top
Inspired by Verner Panton's 'Pop Art' experiments with pneumatic seating, the inflatable PVC Blow was designed in 1968 by Gionatan De Pas.

Above
Gionatan De Pas, Donato d'Urbino and Paolo Lomazzi's Joe glove chair of c.1970 was a tribute to baseball icon Joe DiMaggio and an ironic comment on overpriced leather upholstery.

The philosophy that 'less is more' (Ludwig Mies van der Rohe) was followed by 'less is a bore' (Robert Venturi). Functionalism without delight really wasn't enough. Designers wanted to experiment with new concepts, with designs that clearly broke the rules or were humorous or even comic.

The most influential design group was the Memphis group, founded in Milan in 1981. Its leader, Ettore Sotsass, famously declared, 'A table may need four legs to function, but no one can tell me that the four legs have to look the same.' Memphis designs luxuriated in bright colours, unusual shapes, asymmetry and a quirky sense of humour. Eclecticism became the new muse. The Post-Modern designer was happy to take inspiration from the past – but his use of that inspiration was usually irreverent. The chair could be a happy mix of, say, a Queen Anne chair shape with a theme from popular culture and unusual materials. Robert Venturi (b. 1925) used his chair designs as a symbolic statement, to comment on people's cursory interest in the history of design, showing it to be skin-deep. The overall shape hinted at the historical prototype, while the 'skin' was a modern plastic laminate or veneer.

While the chair designers of the late 1970s and 1980s discarded the principle of 'form follows function', some also ditched the goal of furniture being mass-produced so that it could be sold at an affordable price. Seemingly disposable chairs made from cardboard were sold in high-end galleries. But there was another side to design in the 1980s, with American designers such as Wendell Castle and Sam Maloof producing either very limited-edition or unique pieces in personalized styles that involved high levels of craft.

The Post-Modernism of the 1980s ended as it began – as a reaction to something else. The bubble burst. The end of the 1980s saw a recession and stock markets wobbled. In the more stringent atmosphere the excesses of the past 15 years seemed self-indulgent. In what has been called 'Late Modern' or New 'Minimalism', designers of the 1990s looked back at the Modernist tenets of function and form. Decoration was pared down, and sleek lines were again in vogue. Colour, if used at all, was in solid blocks.

Yet all was not lost from the Post-Modern experiment. Chair designers realized that personality and even eccentricity had a place in modern design. Self-promotion became an important tool of the modern designer. The recycling of found objects played to the concern of the late 20th-century consumer about the damage we are causing to our environment. Craft and technology could now become bedfellows, as computer technology allowed the designer to create ever-more fanciful designs.

To end, I can do no better than quote one of the greatest designers of the 20th century, Mies van der Rohe (1886–1969), who wrote in 1930:

"The chair is a very difficult object. Everyone who has tried to make one knows that. There are endless possibilities and many problems – the chair has to be light, it has to be strong, it has to be comfortable. It is almost easier to build a skyscraper than a chair. That is why Chippendale is famous."

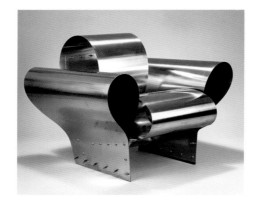

Above
Highly sculptural in appearance, Ron Arad's mid-1980s 'Well-Tempered' armchair consists of four bent and bolted temper-rolled sheets of stainless steel.

Top
Gaetano Pesce's Post-Modern resinous wool-over-plastic I Feltri armchair of the mid-1980s is an 'object of uncertain form' which moulds to the shape of the sitter.

Above
Although of industrial
name and form, Tom
Dixon's Pylon chair
of 1992 is comprised of
lengths of lacquered iron
wire, all hand-welded
together in true Arts
and Crafts tradition.

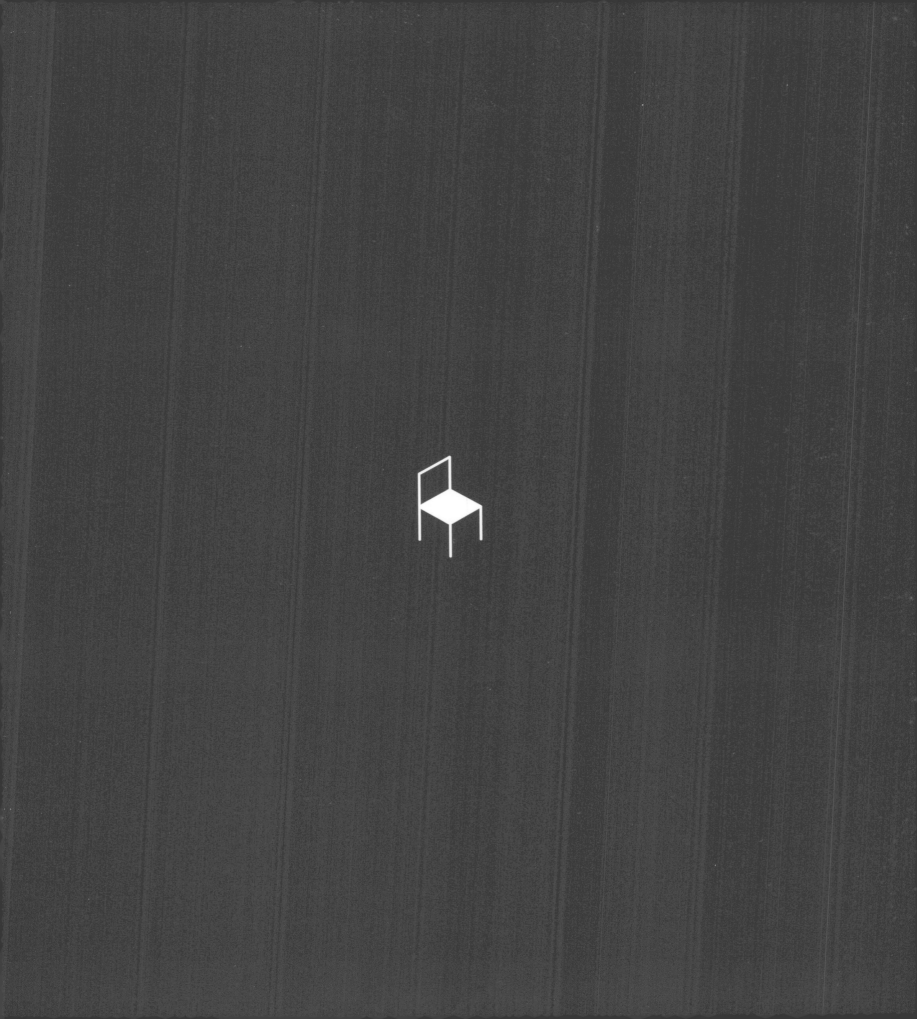

Wainscot Armchair / c.1640

This English armchair was made just prior to the middle of the 17th century, but it is of a type that had emerged more than a hundred years earlier. It is commonly referred to as a 'wainscot' chair because its carved back panel is similar in both thickness and style to the wooden cladding, or wainscoting, often used to decorate the lower section of walls in affluent households during the Renaissance. Technically, however, it is an open-frame joined armchair.

'Open-frame' refers to the fact that neither the sides of the arms nor the front, back and sides of the under-seat frame are enclosed with planks or panels. This feature made the chair less cumbersome and more portable than its immediate forerunner, the enclosed (or 'boxed-in') armchair that had been prevalent in the 16th century. In addition, it helped to secularize the chair, making it appear more domestic and less church-like than its predecessor.

The term 'joined' in the chair's description is also historically and aesthetically significant. It refers to its method of construction, in which mortise-and-tenon joints link the load-bearing components, and the panel back is rebated in a mason's mitre-jointed frame. Originally used by the ancient Egyptians, Greeks and Romans, these jointing techniques revolutionized chair-making when they were 'rediscovered' during the Renaissance. By doing away with nails and bands of iron as connective mediums, they allowed the wood – whether a thick arm, leg, rail or stretcher, or a thinner, wainscot-like back panel – to naturally shrink and expand a bit during changes in temperature and humidity, thereby minimizing the risk of its splitting.

Constructed from oak, as most wainscots were, the chair's frame is raised on four legs. Typically, the rear pair is of plain square section, while the front pair, like the arm supports above them, is ring-turned on a lathe, and all are united by plain rectangular stretchers. Between gently concave arms, the square wooden seat – which would have originally been augmented for comfort with a loose squab or cushion – is additionally supported by seat rails with simple edge mouldings. In contrast, the back is characteristically the most decorative part. Set under a cresting rail carved with blind arcading, it boasts an arch of rosette-enriched guilloche, carved beneath a pair of flower-and-leaf spandrels, and all centred on a single large rosette.

Although not the most flamboyant example – some wainscots, for example, had elaborately carved and pierced, arched or scrolled cresting rails – this robust, pleasingly proportioned oak armchair is of a type that remained both prestigious and fashionable in Britain, northern Europe and colonial North America until the mid-17th century (and later in the remoter rural areas). Thereafter, it was to prove a source of inspiration to some late 19th- and early 20th-century Arts and Crafts designers, but its more immediate fate – as the 18th century beckoned – was for it to be gradually rendered obsolete by new woods, styles and techniques.

Above left
Carved into the chair back, the interlaced bands known as guilloche – here encircling rosettes – originated in Assyrian and Graeco-Roman Classical ornament and were revived during the Renaissance.

Banister-Back Armchair / c.1700–10

This grand armchair was made in Massachusetts, probably Boston, during the first decade of the 18th century. Most chairs made in what were at that time Britain's North American colonies were inspired by recent European forms of seating, and this was no exception.

The European source, although invariably characterized by the use of component wooden parts decoratively turned on a lathe, displayed some regional variations. Many French chairs, for example, had tapestry-upholstered seats and backs, while Spanish and Portuguese equivalents were often of pattern-stamped leather. However, the version that inspired this Colonial American model originated in the Netherlands and became most popular in Britain c.1660–85 during the reign of Charles II – a period from which it acquired the style label 'Carolean' (*Carolus* being the Latin for 'Charles'). The distinguishing feature of these Carolean chairs was their cane-work seat and back panels, so why, one might reasonably ask, the distinct absence of cane in the Colonial version? The answer lies in geography, economics and American ingenuity.

Imported by sea from the Orient, by both the Dutch and the English East India Companies, cane became a particularly *à la mode* component of chair construction during the second half of the 17th century. It also had the virtue of being relatively cheap – but not in the far-distant North American colonies, where the greater costs and uncertainties of cross-Atlantic supply made it a much scarcer and more expensive medium. For Colonial craftsmen an alternative to a cane seat was fairly straightforward: indigenous rush was in plentiful supply. However, that would not do for the back, neither practically nor aesthetically. So, why not simply extend the wood-turning techniques that characterized most of the rest of the chair and, instead of cane panelling, install a run of vertical posts? Turned on a lathe to look like stairway banisters, the innovation proved a sympathetic and elegant solution, and one that gave the American version of the chair the name 'banister-back'.

This particular example is fashioned primarily from maple wood, but also in part from hickory or ash. In addition to the banister back – the individual posts of which are flattened (or 'split') for comfort – the turned components include block-bulb-and-ring front legs and arm supports, ring-bulb-and-baluster stretchers and, above gently curved square-section back legs, block-ring-and-baluster stiles that terminate in bulb-covered-urn finials. To confirm this is a very prestigious chair, these decorative forms are augmented with flourishes derived from Classical antiquity, evident in the scrolled arm terminals and, especially, the magnificent cresting rail carved with C-scroll and scrolling acanthus leaf imagery. The chair also retains much of its original bluish-green painted finish, which is enlivened with gilding on the finials and selected bulbs, rings and balusters. Together, these decorative conceits create a sense of Colonial refinement and grandeur the equal of any British Carolean prototype.

Daniel Marot-style Side Chair / c.1710

Although this walnut side chair – one of a set of eight – was made in England, its design is copied from engravings published by the French Huguenot architect and designer Daniel Marot (1661–1752). In its form and decoration it embodies the late Baroque style pioneered in France towards the end of the 17th century under the patronage of Louis XIV. The fact that this extravagant style in general and Marot's chair designs in particular were adopted in England was an indirect consequence of religious intolerance.

Born in Paris, Marot had become versed in the 'Louis XIV' style as a pupil of the eminent designer Jean Le Pautre and as an engraver of designs by the equally eminent royal appointee Jean Bérain. Following the withdrawal of Protestant religious and civil rights in 1685, Marot fled France for Holland. There, in the employ of William of Orange, he designed a number of state palaces in the full-blown 'Louis XIV' style. After William and his wife Mary had been crowned King and Queen of England in 1689, Marot moved to London and, as royal architect and Master of Works, proceeded to remodel Hampton Court Palace in the same manner. Recorded in engravings published after he returned to Holland in 1698, Marot's designs for architectural fixtures and fittings, furniture and soft furnishings proved hugely influential. Indeed, his side chairs not only were widely copied at the time, but also were often reproduced well into the mid-18th century, and then again during the revival of various historical styles during the 19th century.

The appeal of the Marot-style side chair is readily understandable. With its imperious high back and sophisticated carving, it immediately creates a sense of wealth and importance – an impression enhanced by the warm, mellow patina that the walnut from which it was made has acquired over the passage of time. Numerous aspects of the chair draw the eye, not least the voluptuous cabriole front legs. Of animal form and terminating in hairy hoof feet, they are enriched at the knee with scrolling foliate forms and are united at the front by a double S-scroll stretcher that almost suggests a pair of leaping dolphins.

However, set behind a red velvet-upholstered seat with *campana* (bell-shape) tasselled fringing, it is the back of the chair that provides the primary focus. Flanked by, and mirroring the profile of, subtly undulating channelled stiles, the carved and pierced central splat displays tiers of formalized flowers and foliage within a scrolling border. It rises to an equally sumptuous cresting rail – the latter a serpentine composition of C-scrolls with a scrolling foliate and plumed surmount. Derived, via the Renaissance, from the Classical vocabulary of ornament, all of this superbly carved imagery serves to enhance not only the intrinsic opulence of this Marot-style side chair, but also its enduring gravitas.

Above right
Animal-hoof feet were a fashionable conceit on many chairs in the late Baroque style, inspired by artefacts and furnishings from Classical antiquity.

Queen Anne Open Armchair / c.1710

Made in England early in the 18th century, during the reign of Queen Anne, this chair has many admirable qualities, but arguably the most pleasing, and certainly the most historically significant, are the lightness and openness of its design. With the notable exception of 'wing-backs', chairs in general had been gradually becoming lighter, less enclosed and more portable since the mid-17th century, but these attributes have been taken to a new level here.

To some degree this is owing to the colour of the chair's sturdy frame. The solid walnut from which it is fashioned displays a mellow, yellowish-brown patina that not only is visually light, but also gives the impression of greater physical lightness. In fact, the use of walnut was a little fortuitous. Approximately a year before the chair was made, the exceptionally hard winter of 1709 had destroyed most of Europe's walnut trees. As stocks of seasoned timber dwindled, the use of walnut was increasingly restricted to veneer, rather than solid form as here. By c.1730 it had been largely supplanted by imported mahogany – in most cases a darker and therefore heavier-looking wood.

Of course, the greater lightness and openness of the chair are ultimately due to the form and configuration of the component parts. Below the seat, three of the turned stretchers are of simple slender circular section, while the slim front stretcher is presented in an elegant crossbow shape. The legs are also proportionately slender, and while the back pair curves subtly down into rectangular blocks for greater solidity, the 'show' pair at the front splays more gracefully into out-swept pad feet. The smooth lines and uncluttered look of the under-seat frame are also enhanced by the minimal use of carved decoration – in this case small tobacco plant motifs in relief where the front legs meet the seat rails. Above, each elegant arm terminates in a slightly out-swept 'shepherd's crook', which curves down into a curved arm support set well back from the front of the chair. By easing the access and exit for the sitter, this configuration also helps to open up the chair – again, both physically and visually.

The curves of the 'shepherd's crook' arms are echoed in the rounded seat and the subtly reclined spade-shaped back. Re-upholstered in a 'gros point' needlework fabric, in keeping with the bold foliate and floral tapestry patterns fashionable in the early 18th century, they reveal a more curvilinear trend emerging in chair design – one that would come to fruition later in the century as the Rococo style. Also, the back and especially the seat are generously stuffed, an indication that comfort would be an increasingly important factor in chair design from now on.

Above
'Shepherd's crook' arms (top) were fashionable during the reign of Queen Anne, as was the tobacco plant motif (below), a reflection of an increase in snuff-taking at this time.

Régence *Fauteuil* / c.1720

Historically, the Régence refers to the period in France between 1715, when Louis XIV died, and 1723, when his great-grandson and heir, Louis XV, became legally old enough to rule. During those intervening eight years France was governed under a regent: Philippe, Duke of Orléans. However, when the description Régence is applied to French furniture, as for this c.1720 French *fauteuil*, it encompasses stylistic changes that emerged as early as 1710, were consolidated during the Régence and were finally superseded only around 1730 as the full-blown Rococo style came to fruition.

On the one hand, the Régence style was characterized by a move away from the formal and sometimes rather austere late Baroque classicism that had been in vogue for most of Louis XIV's reign – a style encapsulated, for example, in Daniel Marot's chair designs (see page 36). On the other hand, the Régence reflected the move towards a lighter, more open style of decoration. Fuelling this was the Duke of Orléans's promotion of a much greater informality at court, which he moved from Versailles to his Parisian home, the Palais Royal. Its interior refurbishment, by the Italian-trained French architect Gilles-Marie Oppenord (1672–1742), featured flamboyant designs of naturalistic carved flora and fauna that flowed freely over the *boiseries*. Ultimately, they foreshadowed the development of the overtly curvilinear Rococo style, but in the interim they provided a source of inspiration for the type of carved decoration applied to this Régence *fauteuil*.

Fashioned from beech wood, the frame of the chair retains some of the qualities of its Louis XIV predecessors, notably the overall rectilinear shape of the back and seat; however, forthcoming curvilinear Rococo elements are evident in the cabriole legs, stretchers that are crossbow-contoured (*contour à l'arbalète*), serpentine seat rails, curved arm supports, scrolled arm terminals and feet, and bow-shaped top rail. A low back – less imposing than many of the higher-backed Louis XIV-style chairs, better suited to sitters wearing long, extravagant wigs, and more conducive to informal conversation – adds to the greater sense of openness. This is further enhanced by the cane-work panelling, as well as the set-back arm supports, which better facilitate getting in and out of the chair wearing a hoop skirt or a large frock coat.

While acceptable posterior comfort is supplied by a fitted squab stuffed with horsehair and wadding, and covered in leather, the most appealing aspect of the *fauteuil* is the carving. Although applied to the legs, arms and arm supports, it is at its prominent best where it appears to grow almost organically out of the seat rail at the front and the top rail at the back. Set against a ground of diaper-work tooling, it features a central shell motif flanked by scrolling acanthus foliage and trailing flower heads – all vigorously and crisply carved and impressively naturalistic.

American Queen Anne Wing Chair / c.1745

In the mid-18th century an extravagantly upholstered wing chair was a considerable luxury. For those living in what were at that time Britain's American colonies, even the most basic upholstery fabrics were hugely expensive as they had to be imported from Europe. As a result, the yards of fabric – such as a fashionable silk or woollen damask – needed to cover the large surface area of a wing chair was something only the very wealthy could afford. But what an investment that was: a comfortable easy chair that could be drawn up to the drawing room or parlour fire on a chilly winter's night and cocoon the sitter from draughts within its curvaceous wings. Given the date of this chair's manufacture – c.1745 – it is also tempting to imagine the confidences that might have been shared while sitting in it safe from eavesdroppers. Was this chair privy to political talk, thoughts of rebellion or even revolution?

In terms of form, the depth of the wings and the generous proportions of the seat and high canted back not only provided a level of comfort only money could buy, but also would have made that very evident to any visitor to the house. Sympathetically re-upholstered in the 21st century with a stylized floral pattern red silk damask that would have been highly fashionable in the mid-18th century, the chair's wooden frame – aside from the legs and stretchers – is constructed from maple and undoubtedly made in New England. It is branded with the initials D G, which very possibly stand for Daniel Griffiths, a cabinet-maker working around that time in Portsmouth, New Hampshire.

At that time New England furniture buyers favoured a rather more restrained style of chair than their neighbours further south. However, as this particular chair attests, this did not mean that Queen Anne-style New England chairs were puritanically lacking in attractive detail. Indeed, the sumptuously scrolled wings descending into the splayed cone-shaped arm supports imbue an essentially simple design with what to many eyes is a curvaceous sensuality. This quality is, to a lesser degree, echoed in the chair's short but shapely cabriole front legs. Carved with pad feet they are, characteristically, in marked contrast to the slightly raked rear legs, which are of plain square section and rise up under the upholstery to form the stiles of the frame. Uniting the legs, the stretchers are of a turned block-and-spindle type.

Later in the 18th century, during what is sometimes referred to as the 'late Chippendale' period, all the legs and the stretchers under wing chairs would become straighter and plainer, and during the Federal period the seats and backs would become less generous in their proportions. Apart from that and minor variations in the profile of their wings and arms, the basic style and form of wing chairs remained much the same from the late 17th to the early 19th century, and in numerous historical revivals thereafter – testament indeed to the enduring appeal of a classic design.

American Queen Anne Side Chair / c.1750

The elegance of this American Queen Anne chair owes much to its place of birth. Philadelphia, the largest city in the North American colonies at that time, saw an influx of immigrant cabinet-makers from around 1730, many of them Quakers. Among them was John Elliott (1713–91), who left Leicester, England, for the New World in 1753 with his wife and five children. It is believed that this side chair was made in his workshop on Chestnut Street.

Wealthy patrons paid newly arrived craftsmen such as Elliott, as well as those who were second- or third-generation immigrants, to make furniture in the styles that were being imported from Europe. Their interpretation often resulted in taller, more slender chairs than the examples on which they were modelled. However, fashions changed slowly, and so the taste for the Queen Anne style lasted longer than it did back in England – until around 1760.

In many respects this chair is typical of one made at the high point of the Queen Anne style's popularity in the North American colonies, and is fashioned from walnut. The most popular wood in the Colonies at the time, it gives a rich, lustrous finish when stained and polished – here pleasingly mellowed by the patina of time. In terms of form, the chair's solid vase-shaped splat rises from a horseshoe-shaped seat, which houses a drop-in seat pad and is framed by a yoke-shaped top rail. The crest is decorated with a carved shell, which is characteristically echoed on the knees of the cabriole legs. Both the graceful scrolled splat and the curvaceous stiles and top rail are typical Philadelphia details, while the depth and detail in the carving of the shells reveal a master Philadelphia craftsman has been at work. Such carefully considered sophistication is a hallmark of the designs popular in the city at this time – as is the finely executed trifid foot that terminates each cabriole leg.

Exclusive and costly in its day, a John Elliott chair remains an exceptional piece of furniture. This is partly due to the fact that he stopped making them all too soon: by 1757 Elliot was no longer working as a cabinet-maker and, instead, advertised himself as a 'seller of imported goods' in nearby Walnut Street. The move was a wise one. He is said to have become the major supplier of English-made looking glasses – a business that his son is believed to have taken over when John retired at the outbreak of the American War of Independence. Unfortunately, the Elliot's commercial gain is our loss. Essentially a restrained, elegant and uniquely American interpretation of the exuberant Rococo style, chairs of this provenance are now sadly all too rare.

Above left
The chair's cabriole show legs terminate in out-swept trifid feet. Thought to be Irish in origin, they are also sometimes referred to as drake's feet.

Louis XV *Fauteuil* / c.1755

All chairs are a product of their time, but few, if any, better represent the era in which they were conceived than the Louis XV *fauteuil*. One of the most iconic pieces of all 18th-century French furniture – and much-copied in other countries eager for furniture in the French taste – it encapsulates the significant stylistic and cultural changes occurring in the period between the death of Louis XIV in 1715 and that of his successor in 1774.

In a relatively war-free, prosperous Europe, a major development was the increasingly prominent role of aristocratic women, most notably the Marquise de Pompadour, the flamboyant mistress of Louis XV. With this had come a demand for more informal, elegant and comfortable interiors, better suited to conversation and other pastimes such as reading, music and games. Stylistically, the result was a move away from the formal dignity and heavy Classicism fashionable during the reign of Louis XIV, to the overtly feminine Rococo style. The essential characteristics of Rococo – extravagance, curvaceousness and an accompanying sense of lightness, airiness and movement – are all apparent in the form and decoration of this exceptionally fine *fauteuil*, which was made in Paris c.1755 by the *maître ébéniste* Jean 'Père' Gourdin.

The component parts of the chair frame are, as with many other Louis XV *fauteuils*, fashioned from beech, a wood well suited to carving. Rococo curves, selectively enlivened with flower-head and leaf carvings, are evident throughout, from the S-profile of the cabriole legs, which rise from scrolling acanthus toes, through the serpentine seat rails, to the scrolled elbows of the arms and the cartouche-shaped back. With invisibly pegged joints, these elements combine into a flowing, seamless whole. This quality is further enhanced by gilding, which in a Rococo interior was typically applied 'en-suite' with other fixtures and fittings, such as wall panelling, chimneypieces and mirror frames.

The refined femininity of the design is given a further boost – a very practical one – with the positioning of the arms. Set back from the front approximately one-quarter the length of the side rails, they are designed to accommodate more easily the large, hooped skirts that came into vogue from c.1720 onwards. Equally feminine is the height of the back. Much shorter than the tall, masculine-looking backs of Louis XIV chairs, it is more conducive to casual or intimate conversations from chairs grouped informally, Rococo-style, in the middle of a room, rather than around its perimeter.

The desirability of this Louis XV *fauteuil* goes beyond its appearance, its practicality or its symbolism of a particular period and style. Under top covers of pale green silk velvet with a gaufrage (embossed) floral, leaf and wreath pattern, its generously padded seat, back and arms allow an occupant to entertain or be entertained in considerable comfort.

Left
Each tapering cabriole leg is carved at the knee with a single flower, echoing the beautiful floral decoration of the upholstery and elsewhere on the frame.

Above left
The arms of the Louis XV *fauteuil* are turned slightly outwards and, beyond upholstered armpads, terminate in beautifully carved scrolls at the elbows.

George II Open Armchair / c.1755

The solid, masculine shape of this chair is dramatically contrasted with and lightened by the intricate delicacy of the more feminine Rococo-style carved decoration. To varying degrees, both of these features are apparent in the finest furniture from the mid-18th century in Western Europe, England and Ireland, and it is the degree of contrast as well as the quality of the decoration that enables us to determine the importance of this or any other piece of furniture from this period.

During the 1745–65 era such chairs as this were made plain or fancy according to the wealth and wishes of the patron. Here we see a commission from a wealthy family. The carving to the front cabriole legs and arm supports is exemplary. While the raffle leaves and cabochon motifs to each knee are standard patterns, the scrolled foliate feet are of great rarity, being both complex in design and pleasing to the eye. Such detailing can be achieved only by the use of the finest quality and most expensive timber available. In this case it is West Indian mahogany, which was popularly known as Jamaica wood.

The frame conforms to the established practice of using beech wood for those parts not seen. On fine seat furniture this was less to do with saving money than with using a timber that had the right fibrous structure to receive tacks without splitting. The proportions of the frame are faultless, with the height of the seat enabling the sitter to adopt an elegant attitude in relative comfort, despite the fact that the upholstery adheres strictly to the original severe minimum in order to accentuate the lines of the legs and arms. This has been faithfully re-created by craftsmen using traditional methods, and a top cover of silk woven in France matches closely some remaining 18th-century fragments found on the frame.

There can be no better example to confirm that chairs, more than any other type of furniture, have mirrored the lifestyle of their period. Their angle of back, breadth of seat, and shape and length of leg all reveal immediately the costume and behaviour of the people for whom they were made and thus the period from which they came – no later copy or revival piece has ever successfully emulated the character of this original.

Top right
Centred on a cabochon, superb raffle leaf carving confirms the quality of the chair.

Bottom right
Foliate carving extends down the cabriole leg and terminates in an exceptionally fine foot.

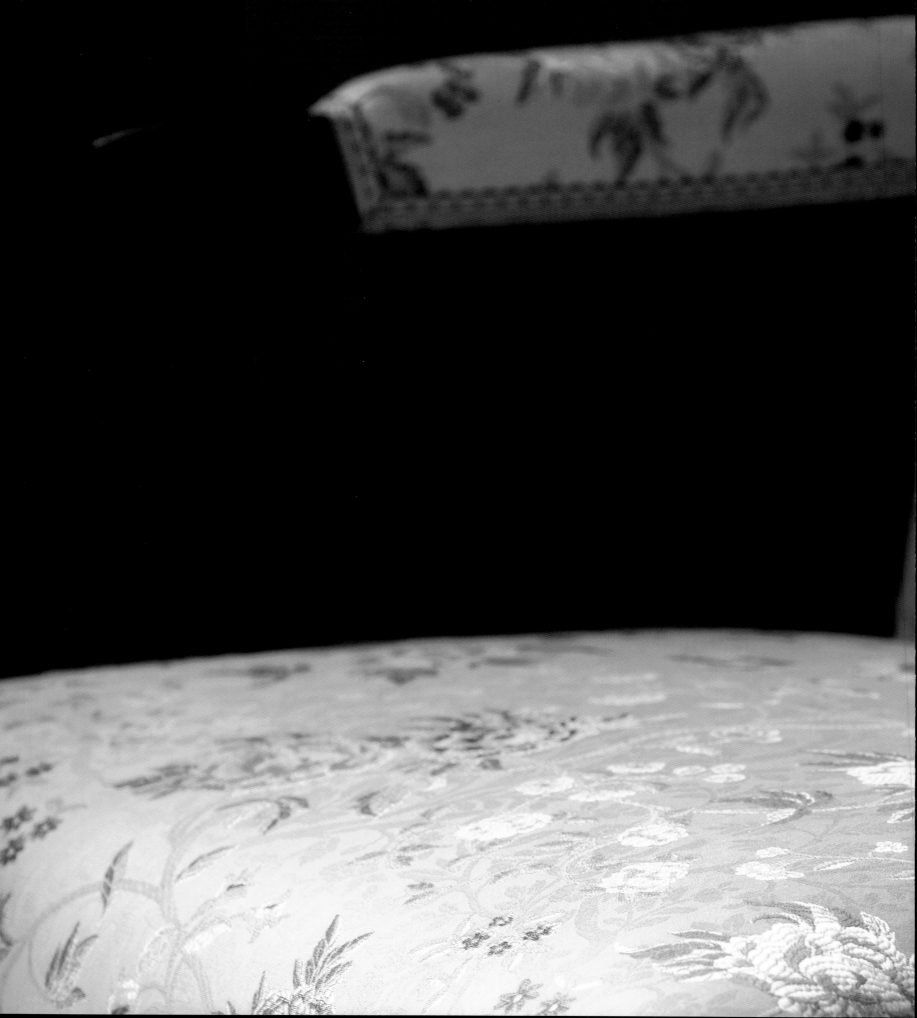

American Chippendale Rococo Side Chair / c.1765

Superior carving and generous curves elevate an American Chippendale side chair from the ordinary to the sublime and prove that less is not always more. When the maker of this chair embellished both its claw-and-ball feet and its knees with elegantly carved hairs, he turned a great chair into an exceptional one.

In Boston and the North Shore of Massachusetts, where this chair was made, delicate claw-and-ball feet with prominent claws were a common feature at the time. The best – like these – feature plenty of carved detail, including individual hairs and sinews.

Even without the added carving, the chair, made c.1765, was already a prime example of its type. The work of an anonymous but highly talented maker, it has an elegantly pierced vase-form splat joined to a yoke-shaped top rail which is crowned by a central carved crest. The upturned moulded ears create a graceful finish to the back, while the cabriole legs have elegant ankles and are joined by finely turned block-and-spindle stretchers. The plain square-section rear legs extend to form the stiles.

By the time that this was made, imported mahogany was the wood of choice for urban buyers. Its dense nature made it ideal for the carved and pierced designs Chippendale promoted, allowing chair-makers to show off their skill. Here it is combined with local maple, which has been used for the hidden parts of the frame.

Elegant and the height of fashion, the designs of Thomas Chippendale (c.1718–79) were the basis for much of the quality furniture made in America in the decade before the American War of Independence. His book of designs *The Gentleman and Cabinet-Maker's Director* crossed the Atlantic soon after its publication in 1754, and colonial craftsmen found themselves imitating his styles to satisfy their wealthy clientele. However, they did not slavishly follow his designs: when Chippendale considered claw-and-ball feet to be outmoded, Colonial makers continued to use them. The result was a stylish interpretation of the new style – not a provincial substitute.

Makers in different regions interpreted the designs differently, no doubt to suit the nature of their client base. In Massachusetts and elsewhere in New England, the conservative buyers were looking for something more restrained than those living further south. The combination of fashionable style and local taste created a style that was unmistakably Chippendale and yet undoubtedly of the New World.

Above
American craftsmen continued to use Chippendale conceits, such as this wonderfully carved hairy ball-and-claw foot, even after Chippendale himself stopped using them.

American Chippendale Gothic Side Chair / c.1775

Even at a time when the English were considered the enemy, wealthy Americans maintained their taste for fine chairs in the latest English style. With its straight front legs and Gothic fretwork, this Chippendale side chair has an undeniably English heritage. It is somewhat surprising, therefore, to learn that it was made in Philadelphia by a maker of Swedish origin.

In late 18th-century Philadelphia, Jonathan Gostelowe (1744–95) was renowned for making furniture that followed English models. One of the city's foremost cabinet-makers, he made high-quality mahogany furniture for a wealthy and discriminating clientele. In a city of great craftsmen, Gostelowe was sufficiently respected by his peers to become chairman of a trade organization called the Gentlemen Cabinet and Chair Makers of Philadelphia, while also finding time to be a Major of Artillery during the American War of Independence (1775–83).

By 1775 Philadelphia's wide, tree-lined streets were home to a cosmopolitan mix of recent immigrants, as well as those whose families had been in the American colonies for several generations. It was a political hub, and Gostelowe's customers were the cream of pre-revolutionary society. At least one of his chairs found its way to George and Martha Washington's home at Mount Vernon, and in 1788 he made a baptismal font and communion table for Christ Church in the city, where Benjamin Franklin, Betsy Ross (who is said to have made the first American flag), the Washingtons and John Adams were among the worshippers.

The relative plainness of the back of this chair is a little unusual for Philadelphia furniture, which tended to be more extravagant than that produced elsewhere in Colonial America. However, the simple treatment lends the chair an elegance that makes it seem superior to fancier models made by his colleagues. Moreover, there is plenty of well-executed detail in this mahogany frame to prove Gostelowe's undoubted skill.

The stiles flare outwards towards the top of the back and are topped by simple ears. They extend beneath the seat into rear legs of near-circular section that flare slightly backwards to enhance stability. The yoke-shaped top rail is supported by a pierced Gothic-style splat, the decorative form of which is echoed in the pairs of corner brackets spanning the front legs and seat rails. The plain, straight Marlborough legs and feet at the front were highly fashionable on both sides of the Atlantic at the time and are complemented by carved linear mouldings along the edges of the legs and around the tops of the feet. Chippendale is said to have based them on a Chinese design. The drop-in seat pad is housed in an essentially square frame which tapers slightly towards the back of the chair. Again, elegant moulding enhances the simplicity of the design.

A chair with these features and of this quality is impressive at any time. But to have been made in the city that was to become the first capital of the United States, by a Major in the revolutionary army about to go to war with Britain, makes it very special indeed.

Right above
The frame of the chair's drop-in seat pad is made of beech – a wood well suited to securing upholstery tacks without splitting.

Right
Of square section, the front legs terminate in what are known as Marlborough feet – a form Chippendale copied from Chinese designs.

Chinese Chippendale 'Cockpen' / c.1775

The fashion for chinoiserie – the fusion of European taste with an enthusiasm for exotic Oriental art – had begun to exert a strong influence on the decorative arts from the late 17th century. It was fuelled in large part by engravings, as well as by the import of porcelain, furniture and lacquer from China and Japan through the thriving trade promoted by the East India Company. Also influential were the designs of the architect Sir William Chambers (1723–96), who had travelled to China with the Swedish East India Company, and the publication in 1754 of the highly influential *Gentleman and Cabinet-Maker's Director* by the cabinet-maker Thomas Chippendale (c.1718–79). Covering a variety of patterns for the household furniture of the gentry, the *Director* captured the popular imagination and made Chinese fretwork synonymous with stylish decorative design during the second half of the 18th century. Indeed, the greatly enlarged 1762 edition of the *Director* contained several versions of a cockpen chair like the one here. A very popular form of chair at the time, it is thought to have later been named after the Chinese-style latticework of some pew chairs found in the Scottish village of Cockpen.

A particularly fine example fashioned from mahogany, and one from a set of four, this Chinese Chippendale cockpen aptly demonstrates why such Western evocations of the Chinese aesthetic proved so attractive. It bears many of the hallmarks of the European taste for chinoiserie typical of the period, but in particular the British penchant for clarity of form. The latter is immediately evident in the overtly rectilinear qualities of the legs and seat, and also in the decorative latticework in the slanted arms and back – in the latter centred on a large octagonal motif. Its panelled mahogany seat was unusual in Western designs at this time, but typical of traditional Oriental chairs and would have been supplemented in use with a loose padded squab covered in sympathy with the rest of the furnishings.

While this cockpen might have originally been intended for use as a dining chair, it is equally probable it could have been part of a grand bedroom suite. Indeed, a spectacular example of this is the Chinese bedroom furniture created by the father-and-son team of furniture manufacturers William (c.1703–63) and John (1729–96) Linnell for the 4th Duke and Duchess of Beaufort at Badminton House, and presently exhibited at London's Victoria & Albert Museum. However, regardless of location in the house, Chinese Chippendale-style cockpens sat well in most fashionable interiors of the era, whether in the flamboyant late Rococo style or the fanciful, romanticized Gothick. Chinese, yet quintessentially British, that stylistic versatility does much to explain its desirability today.

Above left
Fashioned from finely figured mahogany, the cockpen's frame represents 18th-century English cabinet-making at its finest.

George III Faux Bamboo Open Armchair / c.1775

In keeping with the 18th-century fashion for chinoiserie, many European and English craftsmen answered the demand for furniture and ornamental objects in the Chinese taste by creating pieces of furniture, ceramics, silver and glass that featured their interpretation of traditional Oriental designs. They also adopted decorative patterns created by open fretwork, carefully cut reflections of the bamboo plant and cane-work. These techniques were joined by imitation lacquer – known as japanning in England and *vernis Martin* in France for furniture – along with wallpaper, porcelain and tin-glazed earthenware that were embellished with the West's idea of the exuberant Chinese style.

Here we have a splendid example of a mid-18th-century open armchair that has been constructed by a highly skilled cabinet-maker with the single-minded intention of imitating the Chinese furniture traditionally made from bamboo. Derived from the *Bambusa* tree, this wood captured the imagination of Georgian furniture designers on both sides of the Atlantic, who sought to capitalize on the success of the fashion for chinoiserie. Although a sterling paradigm of the 18th-century taste for all things Oriental, this lovely chair made from European woods and carved to simulate bamboo also demonstrates the care taken by these furniture-makers during the early years of the reign of George III. Striving to capture the intoxicating mood that was inspired by Rococo, chinoiserie and Gothick, they paid passionate attention to the detail of these styles, which in concert defined a fertile and prolific period of original and fanciful design.

Along with carving that seeks to resemble bamboo stalks, this chair also boasts a seat made of cane-work, whereby fine strips of the outer fibres of the East Asian palm are closely woven. The technique was first used for the seats and backs of chairs during the Ming Dynasty in China and was introduced into Europe in the 17th century by Dutch merchants trading with their East Indian colonies.

This delightful chair would certainly be at home in a garden setting – particularly in an orangery or the kind of folly that enjoyed enormous popularity in the middle years of the 18th century. Or, combined with matching chairs and a table or two decorated with similar openwork fret patterns, and surrounded by a collection of Chinese and Japanese porcelain and walls covered with Chinese-inspired wallpaper designs of flowers and birds, this chair would be a practical and decorative addition to a more formal room decorated in the chinoiserie taste.

Above right
In a chinoiserie style, the socketed wooden components of the chair frame are turned, painted and clear-lacquered to resemble bamboo.

Windsor Comb-Back / c.1775

Little documented history of the Windsor chair exists prior to the beginning of the 18th century, but a reference to a 'Windsor chair' in the possession of a Philadelphia merchant called John Jones in 1708 indicates that they were made before that on both sides of the Atlantic. It is also known that in Britain they were produced in various locations around the country, including Norfolk, Lancashire, North Wales and the West Country… which begs the question why were the chairs called Windsors? There are various explanations, but the most likely is that the town of Windsor gave its name because of its proximity to the chair-making centres of Buckinghamshire, which had grown up because of the proliferation of beech trees in the surrounding Chiltern Hills. It may also be because of Windsor's proximity to the river Thames, which made it a convenient centre for distribution of the chairs.

Unlike this chair, many Windsors have a shaped central back splat incorporating, two-thirds of the way up from the seat, a pierced spoked wheel. Generally referred to, because of this feature, as wheelbacks, they were introduced in the 1820s. Commonly used in inns, taverns and public houses, they have subsequently become the most familiar form of Windsor chair. They are not, however, the earliest, nor indeed the most desirable. Earlier versions include the hoop- or bow-back, which became fashionable in the mid-18th century, and the comb-back, which is the earliest form, is distinguished by its comb-like top rail and back sticks, and was introduced in the late 17th or very early 18th century.

This chair is a particularly fine mid to late 18th-century example of a comb-back, and is one of a number of well-known stylistic variants. These include 'The Bodleian', named after comb-backs in the Bodleain library in Oxford, and the 'Goldsmith', after the eminent 18th-century Anglo-Irish writer, poet and physician Oliver Goldsmith who owned one. This chair, however, is closely related to one taken on board HMS Resolution by Captain Cook on his final and fatal circumnavigation of the world from 1776–9, and as such is often referred to as a Captain Cook comb-back.

Distinguishing features of the 'Captain Cook' are four turned and splayed legs united by a similarly turned H-stretcher; a horseshoe-shaped seat with a saddle profile; an arm bow raised on an arc of sticks and, at the front, a pair of turned supports; and raised above a stepped intermediate back rail, a comb-back with a shaped comb or cresting rail. All-in-all a model of comfortable, honest support and stability. There is, however, more. Most Windsors were made of home-grown yew, beech or elm. Moreover, many Windsors, especially those intended for use in gardens (sometimes mounted on triangular wooden platforms fitted with three wheels to enable the infirm and indolent to enjoy seated mobility in the great outdoors) were made of green or unseasoned timber to ensure they could expand and contract with less risk of splitting or cracking under extremes of heat, damp and humidity. Not so with this chair, however. It has been fashioned from prestigious and highly expensive imported walnut, rather than cheaper indigenous timbers – seasoned or otherwise. A fitting medium indeed for a Captain Cook comb-back, and one that rather takes the (ship's) biscuit.

Above left
A particularly pleasing detail in the Captain Cook Windsor is the stepped two-tier rail between the top of the arm bow and the base of the comb-back.

Country Ladderback / c.1780

The earliest-known illustration of a ladderback chair can be found in an ancient document in the Bodleian Library, Oxford. Dated c.1338–44, it depicts an English schoolmaster seated in an armchair ladderback while reading with his pupils. Strangely, there is little or no evidence for the chair's use or survival for some three centuries after that – until its re-emergence in Holland in the early to mid-17th century. Thereafter, however, the ladderback has remained a regularly recurring form in the chair-maker's canon and, although almost invariably associated with rural or provincial interiors, it has occasionally crossed over into 'polite' city or urban counterparts.

This splendid example, one of a pair, is English and dates to the last quarter of the 18th century. Cut, turned and carved from elm wood, its component parts exemplify ladderback construction. The most prominent feature is, of course, the back, the four horizontal slats of which resemble ladder rungs, giving the chair its generic name. The number of slats can vary – six is not uncommon – but four is typical. Here they have been cut to a simple cupid's-bow shape, but plainer lunette forms or more exaggerated wave-scroll forms were also employed.

Providing characteristically comfortable support, the slats span the gap between the two vertical stiles. Of turned and tapering circular section, the stiles are – again typically – a continuation of the back legs. Although they are often plain, these stiles have simple ring-turned decoration near the top. This is an 'affectation' you would not find on the well-known late 18th- and 19th-century ladderbacks made in North America by the Shaker community. However, what this chair does have in common with many Shaker chairs is a 'shawl rail': instead of terminating in finials, the tops of the stiles are united by a curved bar. In addition to allowing the chair to be hooked up on a wall while out of use, it enables a loose back cushion to be securely attached with tape hoops.

Secured behind a front seat rail fancily cut to the shape of the slats, the seat is wooden. However, many ladderbacks have rush seats (see, for example, the Arts and Crafts ladderback armchair on page 106–7), a more commonly employed alternative that undoubtedly enhances the rustic qualities of the chair. Under the seat the legs are united at the sides and back by pairs of plain circular-section stretchers. At the front, the single bulb-turned stretcher is far more decorative – as are the front legs. In one of the nicest features of the chair, each leg descends into an elegant slipper foot – an entirely appropriate terminal for a chair that, to echo the words of Shaker Thomas Whitaker, 'achieves beauty through a sense of balance, conciseness, strength (though of delicate appearance) and an enduring simplicity'.

Above
Socketed together (top), the wooden components of the ladderback are cut, turned and carved from elm (below).

George III Tub Chair / c.1780

During the first half of the 18th century, the French aristocracy developed a taste for informal entertaining in spaces more intimate and private than grand state rooms. This prompted a demand for cabinet-makers to supply new forms of comfortable smaller-scale yet still luxurious seating. Thus by the mid-18th century the variety of chairs had increased considerably – a development also fuelled by the seating requirements of the burgeoning middle classes. This phenomenon was repeated throughout much of Europe and Scandinavia, and on the other side of the Atlantic in the North American states, but in almost all cases French prototypes provided, either directly or indirectly, the inspiration.

Of the many popular French chair styles conceived during the 18th century, the *bergère* went on to prove a perennial favourite. It first appeared in around 1725 during the Régence period, when the Rococo style was in its infancy, and, although subsequently produced in various shapes and sizes, it is essentially an easy armchair with an exposed wooden frame; a low back (either upholstered or caned, and often but not always rounded); enclosed sides (this a distinguishing feature and, depending on the back, either upholstered or caned); and a wide, deep seat augmented with a plump, loose squab cushion. The earliest examples also had cabriole front legs, but thereafter various styles of leg were employed.

The *bergère* shown here was made c.1780 during the reign of George III and is a particularly pleasing example of the English interpretation of the French *bergère* form. As such, it is more usually referred to as a tub chair, after its rounded tub-shaped back. All three editions (1788, 1789 and 1794) of George Hepplewhite's influential *The Cabinet-Maker and Upholsterer's Guide* contain plates showing chairs with a very similar outline to this, and it is of a type produced by leading English cabinet-makers such as Seddons of London and Gillows of Lancaster, and very popular during the late 18th and early 19th century.

Much of the contemporary and enduring appeal of the chair resides in its mahogany frame. Overall, it displays the rectilinear qualities associated with the Louis XVI Neo-Classical style, but these have been subtly softened with some Hepplewhite curves: most evident in the top rail which gracefully sweeps down as one with the arms, but also in the out-swept back legs, the fluted baluster-shaped arm supports, and the tapering front legs of fluted circular section and ring-turned about the feet. Well made, robust and sympathetically re-upholstered in a hard-wearing woollen-weave fabric, this chair displays an understated, slightly austere elegance that is perfect for a study or library, and, despite its French origins, is unmistakably English.

Above
The rectilinear qualities of late 18th-century Neo-Classicism are evident in the reeding of the arms, and the fluting of the arm supports and legs.

George III Polychrome-Painted Shield-Back / c.1785

The Neo-Classical style of furniture, popularized in Britain by James 'Athenian' Stuart, Sir William Chambers and especially Robert Adam, had roots in the antiquities that had been unearthed from 1738 in the excavations of Herculaneum and Pompeii. Greek and Roman architecture and the rich vocabulary of classical motifs and decorative devices – urns and perfume burners, delicate swags, fluting and oval medallions, acanthus leaves and palm fronds, and friezes and columns among them – were adopted and re-interpreted for interiors in this fashionable new taste that looked to the Classical past for inspiration.

The airy and graceful version of Neo-Classicism adopted by Robert Adam (1728–92) for his furniture designs in the late 18th century saw chairs become lighter and more delicate than they had been during the Chippendale years. This late Georgian chair is an elegant example of a type boasting a shield-shaped back with a pierced splat and down-swept arms that was introduced by Adam and made enormously popular by furniture designer George Hepplewhite (c.1727–86) in the 1780s. Along with Thomas Sheraton, Hepplewhite is credited with adapting and modifying Adam's original designs for grand houses to answer the growing demand by the middle classes for lighter and more graceful furniture. His pattern book *The Cabinet-Maker and Upholsterer's Guide*, which was published by his widow in 1788, featured more than 300 different designs for elegant but practical furniture. Among them was a finely detailed and delicately ornamented shield-back armchair such as this delightful specimen which, originally, would have been part of a set.

Many of the features associated with Adam as filtered through Hepplewhite's designs are present in the chair. For example, while light-coloured woods were often employed for these chair frames – notably satinwood or a pale walnut – it was just as usual for them to be painted. Here the ground colour is a pale cream hue, but equally popular alternatives at the time would have been pastel shades of blue, pink, lilac, green or grey, and in each case would have been chosen to complement the colours employed for the light and delicate plaster wall and ceiling mouldings, as well as in any woven carpet patterns and other soft furnishings elsewhere in the room.

Equally characteristic of late Georgian Hepplewhite design are the classically inspired decorative motifs delicately hand-painted over the ground colour. Notable among them are the fan at the base of the shield back; the finely rendered strings of husks and Pompeiian-style trellising on the splats and arms; the ribbon-like festoons, beading and feathers around the rim of the shield; and the wheat-ear motifs particularly favoured by Hepplewhite for his shield-back designs. Floral and foliate decoration is also extended to the tops of the tapering but sturdy ring-turned front legs, and to the admirably generous stuffed-over seat. Re-upholstered, like the hand-painted decoration, sympathetically to its surroundings, the current top cover of this splendid Hepplewhite shield-back indicates a drawing room location, but overlooking and with access to a similarly elegant and colourful garden.

George III Louis XVI-style Open Armchair / c.1790

In Europe the middle of the 18th century witnessed the beginning of a reaction to the exuberant curvaceous Rococo style. Underpinning this development were the archaeological excavations at the Roman towns of Pompeii and Herculaneum from 1738, together with publications such as Stuart and Revett's *Antiquities of Athens* (published in 1762), as well as discoveries made by individuals on the Grand Tour. Collectively they brought to light the architecture of ancient Rome and Greece, and thereby provided an extensive vocabulary of ornament for an alternative to the Rococo: the Neo-Classical style.

As was almost invariably the case in the 18th century, the application of this style to furniture was led by French designers, such as Flemish-born Jean-François Neufforge (1714–91) and Jean-Baptiste-Claude Séné (c.1747–1803). For those *fauteuils* produced during the Louis XVI period (1774–92) this meant that curved Rococo chair backs, arms and cabriole legs were gradually abandoned in favour of straighter, more rectilinear forms. The growing demand for pleasurable indulgence was such, however, that these Neo-Classically proportioned *fauteuils* were, if anything, even more lavishly decorated than their Rococo predecessors – their beech or walnut frames either hand-painted en-suite with the boiseries or opulently gilded.

This superb gilded open armchair is very much in the style of those French *fauteuils*. However, it was actually made in England in 1790, during the reign of George III, and as such is typical example of an English Neo-Classical chair inspired by equally superb French prototypes. Similar examples were, for example, illustrated in the widely circulated *L'Art du Menuisier en Meubles* pattern book published by Jacob Roubo in 1772, and it also relates to French-inspired designs by Thomas Sheraton included in *The Cabinet-Maker and Upholsterer's Guide*.

In addition to its obviously elegant and generous proportions, and its green silk damask floral pattern re-upholstery, much of the appeal of the chair resides in the imagery employed for the decorative details. Stand-out features include spiral fluting on columnar stiles, baluster-shaped arms supports and tapering front legs. The latter, like the plainer back legs, terminate in toupie feet, and are topped with stiff leaves. The foliate and floral imagery also extends to the acanthus leaf capitals above the arm supports and the pedestal-like, flower-head carved blocks below – the latter similarly embellished above and below the stiles, which also terminate in flower-head finials.

Augmented with a band of gadroons along the gently arched top rail, this finely carved collation of Classical imagery is simply delightful and, being gilded, nothing short of opulent. Is it any wonder that those eminent arbiters of late 18th-century taste, Henry Holland and his client the Prince of Wales (later George IV), chose furniture similar to this to furnish the Prince's prestigious London address, Carlton House?

Above right
Floral imagery from the Classical vocabulary of ornament embellishes the pedestal-like blocks that terminate the stiles beneath flower-head finials.

Regency Dining Chair / c.1805

Henry Holland (1745-1806) was one of the leading English Georgian architects of the late 18th and early 19th century. He is well-known for the chinoiserie schemes he designed for the Prince of Wales, later George IV, in some of the rooms at Carlton House in London, and at the Marine Pavilion in Brighton. However, his most enduring and influential style lay in the interiors and furniture he designed in the French and Greco-Roman styles – these for many prestigious houses, but most notably for Samuel Whitbread at Southill Park, in Bedfordshire. In so doing he played a major role in introducing French Neo-Classicism into early English Regency furniture design, and that was – as this Henry Holland-style dining chair attests – in marked contrast to the more delicate and refined Neo-Classical style established earlier in the 18th century by Robert Adam (1728–92), and represented in many of the furniture designs of Thomas Sheraton (1751–1806).

Most of Holland's actual furniture designs were never published, and of those that were few have survived. Fortunately, however, they were later represented in a monthly journal entitled *The Repository of Arts, Literature, Commerce, Manufactures, Fashions and Politics*, which was published by Rudolph Ackermann from 1809 to 1828. Better-known as Ackermann's *Repository*, it has given us today a fairly concise and accurate record of the extravagance and indulgences of early 19th century Regency life.

Apart from the overall sumptuousness of its appearance, the first thing to notice about this chair, which is one from a set of dining chairs, is its back. Replacing the by then well-established all-in-one back leg and stile, here an elongated and tapering S-scroll stile appears to 'balance' precariously on either side of the back of the seat frame. Belying its solid construction, and selectively ribbed and gilded, it seems to dare the sitter to lean back into it. Below it, the rear legs, also ribbed and gilded in their centres, curve back sabre-like in a revival of the leg shapes originally employed on the *klismos* chairs of ancient Greece. Form and imagery from Classical Antiquity is also to the fore in the front legs; tapering circular sections feature lobed collars above the feet, and are topped with inverted lotus flowers. Like the collars, these are carved and gilded and echoed on the sides of the seat rails; gilded foliate ornament of Classical origin is also employed at the tops of the stiles.

The chair's loose seat squab – which like the 'push-in' back squab is upholstered in a red, floral-pattern, fine silk-weave fabric – is supported on a panel of canework. First introduced on chairs in Britain during the Restoration period (1660–85), canework had generally fallen out of fashion for nearly three-quarters of the 18th century, but had come back into vogue in the mid-1780s. Even more fashionable, however, is the finish of the frame. Usually, gilded carving would be contrasted with other sections grain-filled for smoothness and then painted a solid colour, most notably black… but not in this case. Here, the non-gilded sections have been painted *faux bois* in imitation of rosewood – a fashionable Regency conceit and one that would have been, on a Henry Holland-style chair, appropriately more expensive than the real thing.

Above left
The frame of the chair is painted with a faux rosewood finish – the rich reddish-brown colours of which provide an appropriately opulent contrast to the selective gilding.

American Federal Armchair / c.1805

Coinciding with the early years of the federal government, the Federal style in the decorative arts reflected the newly independent American citizens' optimism and patriotism for their fledgling country. Promoted by Thomas Jefferson, the country's third President, it was founded on the forms and motifs of ancient Greece and Rome, which offered an inspirational and particularly appropriate model for the architecture and ornament of the new republic.

As the country emerged from the American War of Independence, there was a mood for change in all areas of life. The Neo-Classical trend that had taken hold in Europe in the 1760s did not emerge in the former colonies until around the end of the war, in 1783, and was rarely put into practice until about 1790. When the pattern books by those great English advocates of Neo-Classicism, George Hepplewhite and Thomas Sheraton, did arrive however, they were eagerly studied, and the clean, rectilinear forms found in their furniture designs were absorbed into what would became known as the American Federal style.

As the commercial, intellectual and governmental capital of the young country, Philadelphia by the early 1800s had become known as the 'birthplace of American Classicism', with many new buildings being constructed in the Classical style. The corresponding demand for similarly fashionable furniture saw the number of cabinet-makers in the city expand to meet it. It is estimated that between 1815 and 1830 there were more than a thousand of them, and one of the most talented of these was Henry Connelly (1770–1826). Connelly had arrived in Philadelphia in 1801, and approximately three or four years later was commissioned to make a set of 12 chairs for the city's mayor, Thomas Willing. This armchair is believed to be one of that set. Based on a Sheraton design for a parlour chair, the turned and reeded uprights and legs have all been carved with elegant foliate motifs. The arm supports are also baluster-turned, and the turned and tapering reeded legs feature carved *paterae* and trophies-of-arms, slightly bulbous knees and rounded spade feet. These features are all typical of the chairs made in the Sheraton style by workers at Connelly's large workshop.

The full set of these mahogany chairs would have been time-consuming to produce and costly to buy. On top of the considerable expense of the imported mahogany and the labour costs of extensive carving, contemporary price lists show that the down-swept arms, when made for 'sweep side rails' as they are here, cost three shillings extra per chair. Whether or not mayor Willing deemed the effect worth the extra cost at the time nobody knows, but their graceful sweep in keeping with the rest of the frame is certainly much appreciated now, by sitter and onlooker alike.

Above top
Like the rest of the frame, the arm supports are fashioned in mahogany and are of turned and reeded baluster form.

Above
The blocks at the tops of the front legs are each carved with trophies-of-arms – a fashionable Neo-Classical motif drawn from Roman antiquity.

Regency Gothic Side Chair / c.1810

One from a set of eight, this Regency side chair would have almost certainly served primarily at the dining table. The set may well have been originally accompanied by serving tables fashioned in a similar style. The style in question is the Gothic, or Gothic Revival, which coexisted with chinoiserie and various Neo-Classical styles (Etruscan, Roman, Greek and Egyptian) for much of the English Regency. Strictly speaking, this period ran from 1811–20, when the Prince Regent ruled in place of his father George III, but in the decorative arts it is commonly taken to cover the period from the late 1790s to the end of George IV's reign in 1830.

The late 18th- and early 19th-century Gothic Revival, which drew for inspiration on the medieval vocabulary of ornament, is particularly well represented in this very elegant chair, which is of essentially architectural form. The arched back, entirely hand-carved, incorporates lancets (Gothic pointed windows) divided by turned columns within a turned and reeded framework; the lancets are supported by a pair of brackets, both pierced and terminating in pendant forms also characteristic of the Gothic style. This theme is extended to the front, or show, legs. Each carved from a single piece of timber, they are in the form of three conjoined columns known as triple-cluster columns, an architectural support that was frequently employed in medieval ecclesiastical buildings.

One of the great proponents of the Gothic style during the Regency period was the English furniture designer and upholsterer George Smith (c.1786–1826), whose *A Collection of Designs for Household Furniture and Interior Decoration* (published in three parts between 1804 and 1808) did much to popularize it. Smith preferred oak for the Gothic style, writing that 'mahogany is not to be recommended for this kind of work, which requires wood of a close and tough grain, being in places greatly undercut'. However, his preference for oak is rather undermined by the mahogany frame of this chair, which is admirably 'undercut' and of exceptional quality. Of course, out of sight the seat rails are made from a lesser wood: beech. The stuffed-over seat obscuring them is upholstered with horsehair and wadding for comfort, and has a watered-silk top cover with a broad two-tone Regency stripe.

In addition to its visual appeal and quality of manufacture, this Regency Gothic chair also represents an interesting development in interior design. In its recall of medieval architectural forms, it displays a conscious appreciation of the past, serving as a celebration of its English heritage – at that time a rather new phenomena and one echoed on the national stage in the Prince Regent's significant rebuild of Windsor Castle in the romantic Gothic style.

Above right

The chair's clusters of turned and reeded columns, and pierced brackets with pendant terminals, are characteristic of the Gothic vocabulary of ornament.

Regency Chaise Longue / c.1810

Made in England during the English Regency of the early 19th century, this chaise longue was intended as much for visual display within an integrated interior design scheme as it was for practical, comfortable use. Almost certainly one of a pair, augmented with other pieces of furniture complementary to its style, it would have been placed within a formal arrangement in a drawing room. Although visually striking in its own right, it would have been significantly enhanced in that respect when occupied, as intended, by a reclining female (or two) sympathetically dressed in period style.

The sources of stylistic inspiration for both the chaise and contemporary ladies' fashions come under the broad banner of Neo-Classicism. In this instance they are a mixture of ancient Egyptian and Greek prototypes, as represented in wall paintings unearthed in archaeological digs in southern Europe and North Africa during the second half of the 18th and the early 19th century, and as promoted by one of the great arbiters of early 19th-century taste, Thomas Hope. Showcased in his hugely influential illustrated publication of 1807, *Household Furniture and Interior Decoration*, Hope's house in Duchess Street, London, featured in his 'Egyptian' room similar pieces to this chaise.

The upholstered base and ends of the chaise, and the large buttoned seat squab, have been re-covered in a bright green watered-silk fabric edged with polychrome piping and in keeping with the original upholstery, which would have been colour-coordinated to the rest of the drawing room. Although the upholstery is an essential ingredient, the overriding elegance of the chaise is apparent in its frame. It is made of fine-quality mahogany, rather than less expensive beech (which at that time would have been painted to resemble mahogany or more exotically figured woods such as calamander or rosewood). The chaise boasts two pairs of out-swept sabre-shaped legs, which recall those found on some ancient Egyptian benches and on the better-known Greek *klismos* chairs. They are also sometimes referred to as Trafalgar legs because they came into vogue around the time of the Battle of Trafalgar in 1805.

The tops of the legs scroll out into the form of a lotus leaf, beneath a moulded frieze embellished with a pair of gilt brass *paterae*. The latter, like the lotus leaf – which provides the vegetal model for the flamboyant fan-shaped ends of the chaise – were particularly popular motifs during the Regency period and were also derived from the Egyptian vocabulary of ornament. Now lost to anonymity, the makers of the chaise took the trouble to mirror the carved decoration and brass mounts on its other side. Together with brass casters to facilitate easier manoeuvrability, it confirms that this splendid piece of furniture was intended to be seen from all angles – showcased majestically in the centre of a room, rather than sidelined in an alcove.

Regency 'Grecian-Egyptian' Armchair / c.1815

Made in England c.1815 during the Regency period, this open armchair draws inspiration for its form and decoration from Classical Antiquity. As with the Regency armchair, shown on page 90–1 and also made c.1815, the source is essentially the seating and the vocabularies of decorative ornament of ancient Greece and Egypt. However, while zoomorphic Egyptian imagery is very much to the fore in the other more delicately postured Regency chair, here Greek and Egyptian elements via for attention within a far more robust and imperious frame.

This imperious quality is of some historical significance: the imperial ambitions of France' emperor Napoleon Bonaparte had made a major contribution, on both sides of the Channel, to easing out the earlier, lighter and more delicate form of Neo-Classicism promoted by the likes of Robert Adam (1728-1792) in favour of a more majestic or imperial version of Neo-Classicism, which in addition to drawing on Greek and Egyptian prototypes was heavily influenced by Imperial Roman precedents.

Reference to Roman antiquity is immediately evident in the reeded X-frame front legs of this chair. Although both ancient Egypt and Greece had stools with X-frame legs, the best-known historical precedents were the *sella curulis* X-frame stools employed by Roman senators and magistrates. Here the front legs are united to the rear legs of plain square section with a T-frame turned stretcher. Above the legs the front seat rail is decorated with rosettes, a floral motif often employed in both Roman and Greek ornament. However, the gilded lotus flower heads on the back rails and flanking the tablet back splat are most strongly associated with Egyptian decoration. As to the overall configuration of back and the gently scrolling arms, with the latter descending into baluster-turned supports, this recalls both Egyptian and Greek forms. However, the scene on the hexagonal tablet depicting *putti* is essentially Greek or Roman inspired, and almost certainly modelled on decorative ceramics or wall-paintings unearthed on archaeological digs of Classical Greek sites.

When it was made, c.1815, this chair may well have been described as Neo-Grecian because of a gradual swell in demand for Greek decoration in part a reaction to Napoleon's imperial Roman-like ambitions. However, as closer inspection reveals, Greek, Egyptian and even Roman ancestry is evident in its Neo-Classical design, and clearly such stylistic eclecticism does not detract a jot from it imposing presence and desirability.

Regency 'Egyptian-Grecian' Armchair / c.1815

This exceptionally elegant armchair is one of a pair probably made by the Scottish cabinet-maker William Trotter (1772–1833) – an attribution based on comparable chairs supplied by him to Gosford House in East Lothian, and Paxton House in Berwickshire. Based in Edinburgh, Trotter came to be known as the 'Chippendale of the North', and the sheer quality of this chair demonstrates that it was a reputation fully deserved.

In addition to the cabinet-making skills on display, the materials employed are also of the highest order. The pleasingly proportioned frame is constructed from a fine-grained mahogany, which has acquired a lovely patina over time and is selectively inlaid with pear wood, stained to look like ebony – a conceit also applied to the front seat rail and the paw feet of the front legs and arm supports. The woven cane-work seat would have originally supported a loose squab cushion, stuffed with horsehair and wadding, and finished in a woven silk top cover, probably patterned with a polychrome Regency stripe.

The design of the chair almost certainly has its origins in *A Collection of Designs for Household Furniture and Interior Decoration*, published between 1804 and 1808 by the influential English furniture designer and upholsterer George Smith. One element of the Regency style Smith promoted drew on ancient and Classical Greek ornament, and this is represented here in the painted Greek key pattern decorating the lower rail of the chair back. Far more prominent, however, is the chair's Egyptian component. Derived from ancient Egyptian prototypes, plates 43 to 46 of Smith's publication illustrate the chair's slender and wonderfully carved animal-form arm supports, front legs and feet.

During the Regency period, George Smith was by no means alone in promoting this style. Thomas Hope's *Household Furniture and Interior Decoration*, published in 1807, the earlier *Voyages dans le basse et la haute Egypte*, published in 1802 by Frenchman Baron Dominique Vivant Denon, and the work of French designers Charles Percier and Pierre Fontaine also did much, either directly or indirectly, to promote Egyptian style into Regency consciousness. It would be a mistake, however, to conclude that the desirability of a chair such as this was purely designer-led: the early successes of Napoleon's military campaigns in North Africa, and Nelson's naval victory over the French at the Battle of the Nile in 1798, had also done much to fuel demand for Egyptian ornament on both sides of the Channel.

Above
Echoing in profile the fluid curves of the arms, slender arched supports unite the two rails of the chair back.

'Sheraton-Grecian' Dining Chair / c.1820

While ancient Greek and Egyptian forms are often combined in early 19th-century Regency furniture, this splendid armchair is resolutely Greek in inspiration. It is one from a set of ten dining chairs – comprising eight chairs and two armchairs – made for the dining room of a grand house. Although not attributable to a particular maker, they would have been made in England c.1820. While not an exact blueprint, the origin of their design can be found in a number of Grecian designs by Thomas Sheraton (1751–1806) illustrated in his *Cabinet Dictionary* of 1803. More specifically, however, the distinctive scrolled-tablet top rail in the chair backs appears on what is entitled the Consul chair in Sheraton's later publication, the *Cabinet-Maker, Upholsterer and General Artist's Encyclopaedia*, of 1805.

With its curved-tablet top rail and its out-swept sabre legs of tapering square section, the overall form of the chair's mahogany frame is based on the Greek *klismos* chair. However, in this re-interpretation the outward curve of the legs is significantly less pronounced. Combined with a straighter back, it promotes in the sitter a more upright posture than the original, and one more conducive to dining at a waist-height table. The chair is also designed to be more comfortable. Supported on hidden rails, the drop-in seat pad is generously stuffed with horsehair and wadding, and finished in a silk-weave top cover. The bold two-tone stripe pattern would have been the height of fashion during the Regency period, particularly as it is in red, which was thought especially suitable for dining rooms. As illustrated, the armchairs in the set have the additional comfort and luxury of matching armpads.

The applied decorative imagery is in the form of ormolu (gilded brass) mounts, and all have been cast in forms regularly employed in the Neo-Classical vocabulary of ornament. At the centre of the shaped horizontal splat in the chair back is a pierced roundel in the form of a *patera* (ceremonial dish), flanked at either end by an anthemion (a Greek floral motif based on either the acanthus flower or the honeysuckle). The *patera* motif is repeated in the centre of the front seat rail, flanked by tapering shoots of laurel leaves, which are also employed on the tops of the legs. Although this is essentially an English chair, a Sheraton interpretation of a Grecian design, the use and nature of these ormolu mounts also reflects an awareness of the near-contemporary French Empire style – evidence indeed of the increasingly international nature of design in the early 19th century, despite the prolonged hostilities of the Napoleonic wars.

Right
Curved, scrolled and embellished with ormolu mounts, the tablet-top rail is an Anglicized version of the Greek *klismos* prototype.

French Restauration
Fauteuil / c.1820

In the early 19th century, during France's First Empire, the Neo-Classical furniture promoted by the designers and craftsmen who worked for Napoleon – notably Charles Percier, Pierre Fontaine and François Jacob-Desmalter – was bolder, more austere, larger and more heartily masculine than the Neo-Classical furniture that had preceded it. However, after Napoleon's defeat, the period known as the Restauration – from the restoration of the Bourbon monarchy in France in 1815 until the July Revolution of 1830 – saw designers and cabinet-makers gradually adopt a less severe, less strictly linear and rather more curvaceous style. Chairs, tables, beds and cabinets began to take on softer shapes, and the large gilt-bronze mounts featuring heroic Napoleonic symbols with which Empire furniture had been decorated now all but disappeared.

This small, elegant mahogany-frame *fauteuil* – one of a pair dated to c.1820 – is a beautiful example of the fashionable style that evolved for seat furniture during the Restauration period. Easily moved around, it is in the light, graceful 'gondola' shape that became a favourite of the 1820s. The imposing weight and the sharp, severe lines typical of Empire-shaped chairs have here given way to a more fluid and curvaceous outline, evident in the curved top rail, the scrolled arms with volute-like terminals and the cabriole front legs. The flared sabre legs favoured by Empire designers have been retained, but confined to the back. Decoration is kept to a minimum, with incised fluting and low-relief carving of anthemia on the block supports. The pale sage green and cream silk upholstery featuring a laurel wreath, palmettes and scattered flower heads is typical of the classically inspired Empire-cum-Restauration vocabulary of ornament.

Just as this Restauration *fauteuil* retains certain older Empire elements, so, too, it anticipates imminent new developments in chair design. One of its most appealing features is the supportive shape of its back and seat. Although traditionally upholstered with horsehair and wadding, they are ideally configured for sprung upholstery, which in a bid for additional comfort was to become such a feature of mid- and late 19th-century chair design following the invention of the coiled metal spring. Sadly, sprung upholstery would end up completely submerging what is one of this *fauteuil's* most appealing features: a finely figured mahogany frame.

Equally significant, from a technical and social point of view, is the fact that new, more mechanized techniques for shaping wooden components and cutting veneers have been used in the manufacture of this *fauteuil*. Their primary advantage over traditional methods of craftsmanship was that they enabled cabinet-makers to produce sophisticated wooden shapes quicker, cheaper and in greater numbers. Provided these mechanized techniques were employed, as here, to the same high standards as the traditional methods of craftsmanship, they made luxurious, stylish and comfortable chairs such as this *fauteuil* affordable to the 19th century's rapidly burgeoning middle classes, instead of being, as hitherto, the preserve of a wealthy elite.

Above left
The *fauteuil's* arms descend into scrolling volute-like terminals which, in Classical ornament, were purportedly based on the shape of a ram's horns.

Victorian Hall Chair / c.1860

Although now one of a pair, this fine-quality Victorian hall chair may have originally formed part of a larger set – perhaps as many as eight or even 12 chairs – designed to be formally arranged around the entrance hall of a large house. Probably made in either London or Dublin, the chair is fashioned in a reddish-brown mahogany that has acquired a very pleasing lustrous, mellow patina over the years. It dates to c.1860, although it is of a style that could have been made a decade or so earlier. The style in question is the Gothic Revival and would have been chosen to reflect either the architecture of the house or the design scheme of the hall that it was to occupy. However, as with most Victorian furniture, other vocabularies of ornament are also evident in its decoration.

The principal feature of the chair is its splendid medallion-shaped back, which has been crisply hand-carved with a ring of Gothic tracery, comprising foils and cusps terminating at five points with leaf and berry motifs. At the centre of the medallion is a family crest, in this case a carved bird. A crest was the emblem originally attached to the helmets of medieval knights as a means of identification, and it forms part of a family's coat of arms. Displaying the crest or armorials on the hall chairs of the family to which they belonged was a fashionable Victorian conceit. Interestingly, many hall chairs were carved with spurious crests for families, probably newly rich and with no coat of arms, who wished to give the impression of descent from an ancient line.

Gothic imagery is also extended to the tapering square-section front legs, which are carved near the top on all sides with quatrefoils. However, just above them, running as a frieze along the front and side seat rails, are carved lotus flowers. Also employed where the back rest joins the seat, the lotus motif dates back to ancient Egyptian ornament and reflects the Victorians' fascination with Classical as well as medieval antiquity.

Unusually for most seat furniture, the hall chair was not really designed to be sat on for any great length of time, and in that sense its function was primarily decorative. Moreover, the absence of an upholstered seat or loose squab ensured that any visitor to a house grand enough to accommodate a set of such chairs would remain suitably uncomfortable while awaiting the appearance of the house owner. Indeed, the same thinking probably applied to the only other users of such chairs: the liveried footmen of the household who might sit on them until summoned by their employers. Evidence of this is sometimes present on the seats of hall chairs in the form of small indentations made by uniform buttons – but not on this obviously thoughtfully owned and near-pristine example.

Victorian Feather-Back / 1860s

Some chairs are visually spectacular at the expense of functionality, while others are eminently usable but of nondescript appearance. This Victorian chair, however, is compromised on neither front. It is of a design originally fashionable during the 1870s and 1880s, although the earliest examples date to the late 1860s. This one was made in England, but the inspiration for its design was essentially French. It also proved a popular form in the United States, especially in some of the grander houses of the South in areas with a significant French heritage such as New Orleans.

Although not rare, the chair is of a type not often encountered today. It is usually confined to original period homes or authentically restored interiors, within which its typical location would be a salon or, more commonly, a boudoir. Specific historical precedents for its style are difficult to pin down. Within its overall form there are elements of the late Baroque and the Rococo, and imagery associated with Gothic ornament is also present in its decoration. It could be classified stylistically as 'Victorian Historical-Revival' — with the vagueness that often implies — but, better still, just 'Victorian'.

Undoubtedly the most impressive feature of the chair is its back rest. Although sometimes labelled fan-shaped, and although also resembling an anthemion from the Classical vocabulary of ornament, it is more correctly identified as a feather-back. Employed as heraldic crests in the Middle Ages, feather motifs often appeared in the designs of the French ornamentiste Jean Bérain in the late 17th century and were subsequently copied throughout Europe. They can, for example, be found in the 18th-century Neo-Classical designs of Robert Adam, George Hepplewhite and Thomas Sheraton. Around the same time, on the other side of the Atlantic, the feather motif began to be employed in decoration as an attribute of North America because of its use in the headdresses of Native American tribes. This development in turn resulted in a resurgence of its popularity in France, partly because France was America's ally in the American War of Independence, and partly because of J J Rousseau's romanticization of the 'noble savage'.

In addition to the shape of the five-plume feather-back, French imagery is also on display in the decoration of the mahogany frame. Carved in deep relief, the floral decoration features at intervals the fleur-de-lys, perhaps the most iconic of all French motifs since the Middle Ages. The floral decoration is repeated on the seat rails and augmented with acanthus-leaf carving on the cabriole legs, while more stylistic floral and foliate imagery has been employed in the silk damask covering the upholstery. The latter, stuffed with horsehair and wadding, and combined with a broad, low seat, would originally have provided comfortable support for activities as diverse as conversation, repose, nursing a child or, that most French of activities, an amorous engagement.

Above right
The deeply carved floral and foliate decoration on the mahogany frame features the quintessential French motif: the fleur-de-lys.

Victorian Chaise Longue / 1860s

Made in the mid-19th century, this Victorian chaise longue has an overtly feminine quality that indicates that it was intended for a lady's boudoir or salon. It may well have originally formed part of a suite of salon furniture comprising a sofa, or pair of sofas, up to six side chairs and probably one or two nursing chairs. As such it is a reflection of the large households of the Victorian age and the contemporary fashion for densely furnished rooms. While it is impossible now to attribute the chaise to a particular maker – many Victorian furniture manufacturers produced seating such as this – it is certainly of a design very similar to examples retailed by Heals of Tottenham Court Road, London, from the 1860s to the mid-1880s.

With its three-quarter-length serpentine-profile back, and its single scrolled arm, the overall shape of this Victorian chaise is derived from a form of Regency chaise longue introduced more than 50 years earlier. There are, however, significant differences. First, the Regency antecedent would have displayed carved show wood at the side of the arm, and in the form of a frieze around the seat and a top rail along the back. In contrast, the entire frame of the Victorian chaise is obscured with upholstery. Secondly, while the upholstery of the Regency chaise would have comprised horsehair stuffing with trim layers of wool or cotton wadding, the Victorian chaise typically augments these with a network of springs. The result is not only a softer and, theoretically, more comfortable seat, but also a plumper, more voluptuous appearance – further enhanced by the equally characteristic deep-buttoning of the back and the arm.

Of a generous and open form that could comfortably accommodate Victorian ladies dressed in the large, voluminous skirts fashionable at that time, the chaise is currently covered with a cotton damask in a floral and foliate pattern. It may have originally been covered in velvet, another favourite top cover for upholstered Victorian furniture. Regardless of the type of fabric, it would have been chosen to harmonize with, if not exactly match, the other soft furnishings in the room.

While the chaise's obscured frame is made from beech wood, its exposed legs are carved-turned from walnut, and raised on brass casters to aid manoeuvrability. Although more bulbous, the shape of the legs recalls Neo-Classical French prototypes found on Louis XVI furniture of the late 18th century … and partly, therein, lies the eventual demise of this form of Victorian seating. The mixing of Louis XVI-style legs with a Regency form and Victorian upholstery displays the stylistic eclecticism that so irked the more 'design-purist' Arts and Crafts movement that emerged during the second half of the 19th century. Of course, with hindsight this criticism is rather ironic: the sources of inspiration may have been eclectic, but the result, as this chaise admirably demonstrates, was a distinctive style in its own right, and one that was and is quintessentially Victorian.

Above left
The arm and the back
of the chaise longue
are deep-buttoned
and pleated – a
fashionable convention
on upholstered
Victorian seating.

Arts & Crafts Ladderback / c.1870

Like the George III country ladderback on page 68, this ladderback armchair could date to as early as the late 18th century. Its form, style and method of construction are all compatible with some rural English chair designs of that period. In fact, it was made almost a century later, c.1870, and is an excellent example of a rustic Arts and Crafts chair.

A reaction to the stylistic eclecticism and poor quality of machine-made mass-produced Victorian furniture, the Arts and Crafts movement had been founded in the mid-19th century. Led by William Morris (1834–96), it promoted a return to pre-industrial methods of craftsmanship, and one strand of that lay in revitalizing the traditional 'workaday' furniture designs of village craftsmen. Morris's own furniture company produced a chair rather like this one. Known as the 'Sussex', it differed in its use of canted arm supports and a less comfortable spindle-back, but other than that its rural heritage is very similar.

The frame of this chair – maker unknown – is made of ash and is stained a dark blackish-brown hue which, prior to fading over time, would have given the chair the rather smart appearance of being ebonized. Its four legs, all of simple circular section, were turned on a lathe by hand, as were the eight stretchers uniting them, each pair being alternately staggered in height to improve the solidity of the frame. Greater rigidity is also provided by socketing the arm supports through the seat rails and into the stretchers below.

Functionality, a recurring feature of traditional rustic furniture, and one of the central tenets of Arts and Crafts philosophy, is evident in the configuration of the arms – the fact that they are set back from the front makes it easier to get in and out of the chair. The seat is hand-woven from that exclusively rustic material, rush matting. When dampened for twisting and weaving, it smelled unpleasant enough to give rise to the old country saying 'you could smell a matter a mile off', but dried *in situ* it provides an odour-free and surprisingly comfortable seat.

The admirable qualities of the chair are not confined to comfort, strength and ease of use. Beneath a plain curved top rail, the three graduated slats of the ladderback do offer good support, but they also provide an artistic flourish. In an industrial age when the traditional countryside was often seen as a romantic idyll, it is charmingly appropriate that the slats have been cut in the shape of that most romantic of motifs: a cupid's bow.

Above
To strengthen the chair, the turned, baluster-shaped arm supports are socketed through the seat rails and tapered into the stretchers below.

Victorian Queen Anne Revival Side Chair / 1880s

With its finely shaped uprights, curved back-splat, and cabriole front legs joined by turned stretchers and descending to pad feet, this chair is of a design associated with the reign of Queen Anne and a date of around 1710. In fact it was made 170–180 years later, during the last quarter of the reign of Queen Victoria. This period witnessed a tremendous revival of interest in various historical styles of furniture, notably those of the Renaissance, 18th-century Rococo and Neo-Classical and, as here, the late Baroque style.

The basic form of the chair, which is one of a pair, owes much to the designs of the French Huguenot architect and designer Daniel Marot (see page 36). With its ivory inlay on the back-splat and on the knees of the cabriole legs, the chair's makers – Howard & Sons of Berners Street, London – have also tipped their hat to the seaweed marquetry popular on furniture during the late 17th century. The style and content of the decorative imagery employed – elaborate, grotesque-like strapwork filled with foliate scrolls, flower heads and shell motifs – are also in keeping with late 17th- and early 18th-century Classical conceits, as is the bold scrolling foliate and floral pattern of the red damask top cover of the drop-in seat pad. And yet this chair is no slavish historical copy: there are other, more contemporary influences present.

The first of these is apparent in the sheer precision of the inlay work and the carved components. These were done not by hand, but by machine – often a pejorative description of industrialized Victorian craftsmanship, but not in this case, as the work is of an exceptionally high standard. The second contemporary influence is evident in the fact that Howard & Sons (still in business today) made high-quality, fashionable furniture for an affluent Victorian clientele at a time when the British Empire stretched around the globe. The jewel in the crown of that empire was India, and it is no coincidence that rosewood (for the chair frame) and ivory – both indigenous to India – have been used. Indeed, viewed in this light, the style of the inlay work recalls not only late 17th- and early 18th-century European prototypes, but also exotically inlaid Indian furniture. In this respect, this side chair represents a very clever fusion of styles and influences, and at the same time encapsulates a sense of Anglo-Indian exoticism fashionable in Britain in the late 19th century and still alluring today.

Sheraton Revival Corner Chair / c.1890–1910

This exquisite little corner chair was made in the late-Victorian–Edwardian era, and was inspired by the work of one of the great triumvirate of 18th-century English furniture designers, Thomas Sheraton (1751–1806) – the other two being Thomas Chippendale and George Hepplewhite. Sheraton had published for his contemporaries and for posterity a number of publications illustrating, often in considerable detail, his designs for chairs and other furniture. Some one hundred years on, a Victorian–Edwardian manufacturer could have had access to the four volumes of Sheraton's *The Cabinet-Maker and Upholsterer's Drawing Book* from the 1790s, as well as *The Cabinet Dictionary* of 1803 and the first volume of *The Cabinet-Maker, Upholsterer and General Artist's Encyclopaedia* from 1805. There is, however, no specific design for this corner chair in any of them… which does, therefore, beg the question, why is it described as Sheraton Revival?

The explanation partly resides in the fact that the Victorians and Edwardians, when making 'historical-revival' furniture such as this, usually adopted a non-purist approach, often employing just some of the elements of a style and frequently combining them in the same piece with elements of another style (as with the historical-revival wing chair on page 112). In this case the chair's rounded back and serpentine front seat rail certainly are not Sheraton. Indeed, he is particularly known for chairs with straight or angular backs. In contrast, the three show legs of the chair are very Sheraton. Of square section, each tapering down to a spade foot, they display that rectilinear quality characteristic of late 18th-century Neo-Classical Sheraton forms. It is, however, the inlaid decoration of the chair that ensures no description other than Sheraton Revival will do.

The most extensive use of inlay work on the chair's mahogany frame is in the form of banding executed in bone. On the legs it has been employed to create 'panelling', a particularly fashionable conceit on Neo-Classical furniture of the 1780s. Elsewhere it has been used to track the contours of the front seat rail, the curved and tapering arm supports, and the curved and bowed top rail. Single lines of inlay also appear in the arc of subtly concave ribs that raise the backrest above the seat. In all areas, the overriding purpose and effect of this is to accentuate the graceful, slender form of the chair, in its component parts and as a whole. Although still form-defining, the cartouche of bone and fruitwood inlay at the centre of the bowed back is less architectural than the banding. Acknowledged in the bolder leaf-and-flower pattern of the chair's woven silk re-upholstery, this composition of delicately scrolled and trailed foliage with berries is equally Neo-Classical and equally Sheraton.

Above
The chair's bowed mahogany back is decorated with a Neo-Classical foliate cartouche inlaid with bone and fruitwood.

Historical Revival Wing Chair / c.1890–1910

This armchair is of a type that first became popular in the 17th century, and the mid-18th century American Queen Anne wing chair described on page 46–7 is one of its illustrious predecessors. However, there are combinations of elements in its design that date this chair unmistakably to the late-Victorian/early-Edwardian period.

There are references to winged chairs dating from the late 16th century, although none of these are known to have survived. From the mid-17th century they are referred to as 'easie' or 'cheeked' chairs, and were highly commended for their benefits to the sitter in protecting the head from cold drafts – a feature of most rooms in the winter months prior to the advent of 20th-century double glazing and central heating. Although the basic winged form has remained essentially the same ever since, there have been a number of stylistic changes associated with different historical periods, and therein lies the fundamental appeal of this chair. Rather than replicate a style from a specific period, its Victorian-Edwardian maker's have cherry-picked the best bits from different historical styles, to produce a Historical-Revival style in its own right. In the late 19th century such stylistic eclecticism was criticized by followers of the Arts and Crafts movement, who adopted a more purist approach to design, but in this case were plainly misguided.

Of many stand-out features, the most prominent is the configuration of the back and sides. Under an arched top rail the subtly canted back is enclosed by fancily scrolled and outwardly splayed wings, or cheeks, which descend to rolled arms that terminate in sloping, out-splayed C-scrolls. The same or very similar profiles were originally found on Carolean- or Restoration-style wing chairs fashionable in England during the reign of Charles II (1661–85). They were also employed on some William and Mary chairs (1689–1702), as was the distinctive shaped frieze below the chair's front seat rail. In contrast, the chair's cabriole front legs are derived not from the 17th, but the 18th century. Under shell motifs crisply carved on their knees, they terminate in wonderful ball-and-claw feet – a Georgian innovation inspired by Chinese imagery in which a mythical sacred pearl is held in a dragon's claw.

While these show-wood legs are carved in walnut, the rest of the frame is beech. This is the traditional timber, proved to be the most suitable for the securing tacks, as it was strong enough to take them in close proximity without splitting, but not so hard as to resist and shake the frame when they were hammered home. Such seemingly minor issues become significant when one considers the extent to which the visual impact of the chair relies not just on shape and carved decoration, but also on the competence of the upholster to seamlessly follow the tortuous curves of the frame without forfeiting the comfort required from an 'easie' chair.

Talking of comfort, most upholstered Historical-Revival chairs of this period adopted the more modern technique of stringing the webbing supports under the frame to allow the use of coiled springs – introduced in the 1830s – below the seat cushion. However, this chair, being true to its origins, dispenses with springs and has the webbing strung above the seat rail to support traditional horsehair and wadding upholstery… just so much better for the posture!

Thonet Bentwood Armchair / 1890s

Most developments in chair design are as much derivative as they are innovative. A few, however, are truly revolutionary. Manufactured in the 1890s, this armchair falls into the derivative category, but only because the chair from which it was modified – Thonet's bentwood No. 14 – was very much an example of the revolutionary when it first saw the light of day some 30 years earlier.

Trained as a traditional cabinet-maker, Prussian-born Michael Thonet (1796–1871) first experimented with new methods of bending solid wood for chair components as early as the 1830s. By 1841 his technique of softening the wood with steam and moulding it permanently to shape using mechanical presses proved sufficiently impressive to attract a commission from the Austrian Chancellor Metternich. The appropriately curvaceous bentwood furniture Thonet designed for the grand Rococo staterooms at the Palais Liechtenstein was followed, in 1842, by an international patent that protected his 'chemical mechanical methods' from imitation. The revolution then really gathered pace in 1853, when Thonet and his five sons set up their own furniture manufacturing company, Gebrüder Thonet, in Vienna, and was crystallized in 1859 with the appearance of the No. 14.

Originally designed for the Daum coffee house in Vienna, the No. 14 went on to sell some 15 million units worldwide by the end of the 19th century, and is still in production today. It looks very similar to its author-preferred offspring shown here, but is without arms, the circumference of its seat near-perfectly circular and less generous, and the seat itself either of cane-work or wood. Both chairs, however, encapsulate in their construction and style the bentwood revolution. Take away the arms and the seat panel from the No. 14, and there are just six wooden parts, all in beech wood: a near-circular seat frame; a near-circular stretcher; a hoop back-splat; a one-piece back-legs-stiles-and-top-rail; and two front legs.

Moreover, instead of being joined with complex cabinet-making joints, such as mortise-and-tenons and dovetails, the chairs are all secured together with simple nuts and bolts inserted through pre-drilled holes. Such a simple method of construction was ideally suited to factory-line assembly and to easier transportation for assembly elsewhere. Thereby keeping the costs down, it also made these chairs affordable – a revolution if not by the people, then certainly for them. It also pioneered, well ahead of its time, the flat-pack self-assembly furniture phenomenon of the late 20th century.

Ingenuity of manufacture and affordability would have counted for little, however, if the chairs hadn't looked any good. With or without arms, the aesthetic here is curvaceous but open and uncluttered, indeed almost spartan – making it at odds with much of Victorian style, but uncannily prescient of 20th-century Modernism.

Thonet Chaise Longue / 1890s

The Austrian firm Gebrüder Thonet designed a number of chaises longues between about 1880 and the early 1920s. These include a c.1883 version similar to the chaise shown here, but raised on a pair of arched rails as a rocking chaise, and a 'reclining couch' of c.1920, which rocked back and forth on iron bands. This particular example, however, dates from the early 1890s and is considered by many to be the most elegant and, indeed, the most usable.

The framework of the chaise is assembled from Thonet's signature material: steamed and press-moulded lengths of bentwood beech (see also Thonet's bentwood armchair on page 114). In its overall form, it recalls an aristocratic sleigh which, augmented with fur wraps and a team of dogs, would not have been out of place in the winter snows of St Petersburg or the pages of a 19th-century Russian novel.

Stylistically, the base and the arms also bring to mind the scrolling forms of early to mid-18th-century Rococo ornament – a not overly fanciful notion, given that Michael Thonet (1796–1871), the firm's founder, had designed bentwood furniture for the grand Rococo staterooms of Vienna's Palais Liechtenstein in the early 1840s. In fact, the stylistic inspiration for these elements is almost certainly more contemporary and to be found in the designs of the late 19th-century Art Nouveau movement (Jugendstil in Austro-Hungary and Germany). The scrolling forms do indeed have an organic quality reminiscent of sinuous, undulating Art Nouveau plant-form imagery, and that is entirely appropriate for a chaise so often employed in conservatories and, during the summer months, outside in the garden.

Equally appropriate in that context is the use of lightweight but supportive cane-work panelling for the ergonomically curved seat and back rest – linked via a piano hinge and adjustable on ratcheted bars from nearly upright to almost fully reclined. As a component of furniture, cane appears more garden room than drawing room, more rural than urban. In this case, however, that is a little ironic, as the chaise in its component parts and nuts-and-bolts assembly is an object of industrial production … and therein lies a further irony. The late 19th-century Thonet bentwood chaise longue was to be the precursor of the iconic chaise longue B306 of 1928 (see page 162) by Le Corbusier, Pierre Jeanneret and Charlotte Perriand. Doffing their caps to the bentwood chaise, and with Thonet again the manufacturer, they substituted chromed tubular steel for wood, and leather or canvas for cane, and in so doing ushered in the machine age.

Above left
Fashioned from steamed and press-moulded bentwood, and fitted with cane panelling, the frame is screwed and bolted together.

Argyle Street Tearooms Chair / 1897–8

'Iconic' is probably an overused word nowadays, but if only one chair were allowed the appellation this one could present a very strong case. Designed in 1897–8 by Charles Rennie Mackintosh (1868–1928), it was created for the Luncheon Room of Kate Cranston's Argyle Street tearooms in Glasgow, Scotland.

Not only was this Mackintosh's first major furniture commission, but it was also his first design for a high-backed chair. The high back would have served no real purpose other than to present a sentinel-like presence in the high-ceilinged room for which it was intended – but by making a virtue of necessity Mackintosh created a landmark in chair design. Because of the hard wear the chair would be subject to in a busy tearoom, it had to be sturdy and robust, so oak was a sensible wood to choose for the frame. Originally it would have had horsehair-stuffed upholstery, or rush seating, but in either case it was not intended to be overly comfortable, as one would not want one's customers dallying too long when new customers needed to be seated.

Although the chair is made from dark-stained oak and has an Arts and Crafts 'presence', there is no real historical precedent for its extraordinary construction. The oval top rail tapering towards the edges gives it an aerodynamic feel – appropriately, as it is also pierced with a flying-bird motif. This top rail also serves as a headrest that is slotted into the slender uprights without the use of glue or dowels. Mortised into the headrest are two plain, broad back-splats, which rise from a solid panel connecting the back legs. The panel is arched on the lower edge to reflect the curve of the headrest and the arched seat rails. Between the slightly tapered front legs, and between them and the back legs, double rod stretchers are employed to enhance stability. One unusual aspect of the chair's construction that is not immediately obvious is the profile of the two stiles. Rising as legs from the floor, each is of rectangular section, but on their vertical journey they gradually morph into a broad oval, then at the top narrow to circular section.

Kate Cranston, who was to prove Mackintosh's most supportive client, owned and ran a chain of Glaswegian tearooms, all of which Mackintosh designed or restyled during their 20-year association. She gradually gave him more and more artistic freedom in their design and furnishing, eventually allowing him to come up with the entire design concept. He thus supplied the tearooms with everything from the furniture, light fittings and wall decorations to the cutlery and even the waitresses' uniforms. In contrast, that early Argyle Street tearooms commission, being only for the furniture, was more restrictive and less lucrative … but not in the long run. Mackintosh was able to utilize on later chairs many of the features he introduced for the Argyle Street chair – including the emblematic top rail, the flying bird motif, and the exaggerated height of the back. Over and above that, however, his revolutionary design was soon published and exhibited far and wide, not only establishing his design credentials for posterity, but also having a major impact on designers abroad, notably Austria's Vienna Secession … iconic indeed!

Above
The chair's unique top rail also serves as a headrest. Of ovoid form, it slots neatly into the flanking stiles and is secured with neither dowels nor glue.

French Art Nouveau Side Chair / c.1900–03

One of the most appealing aspects of the Art Nouveau movement of the late 19th and early 20th century is the fact that under one broad stylistic banner it actually gave rise to a number of quite distinct 'sub' styles. For example, the overtly linear forms of Charles Rennie Mackintosh's chairs (see pages 120 and 134) are in marked contrast to the sensuous curves of many French designs, including Louis Majorelle's (see page 126). Although French himself, Léon Jallot (1874–1967) was one of a generation of young designers who reacted against what they considered to be the overly convoluted, heavily moulded curves (the 'macaroni style') of earlier French Art Nouveau, and instead promoted less exaggerated forms and more restrained decoration – qualities immediately evident in the Jallot side chair made around the turn of the 20th century.

Underpinning the nicely understated elegance of the chair, and its desirability, is Jallot's impressive CV. One of the few Art Nouveau designers trained as an *ébéniste*, Jallot had been making furniture since he was 16. From 1898–1901 he managed the furniture workshops of Siegfried Bing's famous retail shop L'Art Nouveau, in Paris, which had opened in 1895, and while there he supervised the preparations for the Bing pavilion at the 1900 Paris Exposition Universelle, which showcased the Art Nouveau style on the international stage. The following year (1901) Jallot became a founding member of the first salon of the Société des Artistes Décorateurs, and two years later established his own decorating workshops, designing not just furniture, but also screens, carpets, tapestries and textiles, and even glassware.

Fashioned from walnut, which displays warm honey tones and a mellow, lustrous patina acquired over the passage of time, the chair frame comprises four subtly out-splayed legs, with the rear pair bifurcated to create arched supports for greater stability. The subtle curvaceousness, inspired throughout by organic plant forms, is echoed in the front seat rail, which is subtly serpentine in profile, and the pierced stiles of the back. Flanking an upholstered centre panel they are pierced and carved in relief with floral and foliate ornament. Significantly, the carving – echoed on the front seat rail – is far less florid than on many French Art Nouveau chairs. Moreover, despite being impressively realistic in most respects, the flowers also have a stylized quality when viewed flat-on. This was akin to many Art Nouveau textile patterns of the time and is more graphically evident in the stylized plant-form pattern of the woven silk fabric with which this pleasingly proportioned and eminently usable Jallot chair has been sympathetically re-upholstered.

Above top
The Art Nouveau vocabulary of ornament is here in the form of floral and foliate imagery exquisitely carved in relief.

Above
Naturalistic foliate carving is extended to the front and, as here, side seat rails and arched supports.

French Art Nouveau Armchair / c.1900–03

It is immediately apparent that nature and organic growth, two major sources of inspiration for the Art Nouveau style, are present in the design of this chair. This is not surprising, given it was created by Louis Majorelle (1859–1926), the undisputed master of French Art Nouveau furniture. Trained as a painter under Millet at the Ecole des Beaux-Arts in Paris, Majorelle had returned to Nancy in 1879 to run the family cabinet-making workshop on the death of his father, and by the turn of the century had become the principal producer of Art Nouveau furniture in France. In 1901 Majorelle also became one of the co-founders of the Ecole de Nancy, which helped to make the city a hotbed of innovative designers, rivalling Paris in its impact on the decorative arts of the period.

Although a decision in 1908 to industrialize the Majorelle workshops resulted in a notable drop in quality thereafter, prior to that period Majorelle's furniture was made largely in accordance with the long-held traditions of French cabinet-making and was thus of an exceptionally high quality. Sturdy and comfortable, this armchair is a typically superb example. Fashioned in walnut, its frame displays a rich, warm, mellow patina and is so beautifully carved that one could almost believe it had simply grown like that. For example, the slightly swollen feet resemble bulbs from which vigorous stems rise and gradually unwind upwards, as would a plant seeking the light. They curve and twist and bifurcate on the armrests to form new stems, eventually terminating in realistically carved poppy seed pods as finials flanking the top rail – other plant form motifs favoured by Majorelle included orchids, water lilies and chicory leaves.

The sculptural qualities of the carving reflect the great care over visual details that Majorelle lavished on his chairs and other furniture. Sympathetically re-upholstered in a plain pale green plush fabric, this particular chair is less flamboyant than some of Majorelle's designs, which incorporated marquetry work, metal or mother-of-pearl inlays, or gilt-bronze mounts. Understated elegance is, however, invariably charming and underpins the attraction of this chair, as indeed does its subtle sensuality. Sitting in it, with your arms resting on its sinuous supports, you are compelled by the tactile qualities of the carving to stroke the walnut and contemplate the nature of true craftsmanship.

Above
Exuberantly carved, each stile of the chair back twists up stem-like to a finial in the form of a cluster of poppy seed pods.

French Art Nouveau Armchair / c.1902–03

It is most impressive that such a striking chair should have been conceived by a designer, Jacques Grüber (1870–1936), who is best-known for his stained glass. Indeed, he could be fairly described as France's most famous and prolific stained glass window designer, whose numerous prestigious commissions included the glass roof of the Galeries Lafayette in Paris. If this wasn't enough, he also designed conventional glassware (most notably for Daum), ceramics, textiles, embroideries, posters, book covers, and was also responsible for designing the lighting for the luxury transatlantic liner Île de France. It is surprising he had time to design furniture as well, but as this armchair demonstrates, we should be grateful for that.

Despite the fact that he later went on to embrace the Art Deco movement, Grüber was primarily a purveyor of the turn of the 20th-century Art Nouveau style – the style in which this chair is fashioned. Grüber's credentials in this respect are impeccable and as impressive as the breadth of his design skills. He had studied at the École des Beaux-Arts in Paris, under the Symbolist painter Gustave Moreau, and he exhibited regularly at the Paris salons. Yet he also taught at that other hotbed of Art Nouveau design, the École des Beaux-Arts in Nancy, for a considerable period of time.

The primary source of inspiration for all Art Nouveau designers was the organic forms of nature. However, some adopted a more representational approach that often included, especially during the 1890s, the use of rich and naturalistic floral and pictorial decoration; on furniture this would usually take the form of intricate carving and/or sophisticated marquetry work. In contrast, other designers developed a more stylized, graphic style, which in furniture sometimes became overtly sculptural. Some of Grüber's pictorial stained glass work embraces the former representational style, but his furniture, and especially this chair, is very clearly in the latter camp.

First exhibited at the 1903 Éxposition d'École de Nancy in Paris, the chair has a carved mahogany frame which displays a curvaceous fluidity that suggests stem- and tendril-like plant forms. Flanking the mushroom-domed upholstered seat, the arms encapsulate Art Nouveau's signature whiplash curve – a sinuous, exaggerated plant-form motif that really comes spectacularly alive when viewed in profile (see the following pages). The slightly out-splayed legs both represent and provide strength and stability, while the upholstered, shield-shaped back-splat is secured to the stiles and arched cresting rail with radiating spars – an almost web-like configuration with a tensile strength that, like the rest of the frame, so effectively captures the essential vigour and vitality of nature.

Calvet / 1902–03

This chair is unmistakably the work of the Spanish architect and designer Antoni Gaudí (1852–1926) and is a masterpiece – albeit a unique one – of the Art Nouveau furniture fashionable in Europe in the late 19th and early 20th century. It is in fact one of a number of pieces Gaudí designed for the Casa Calvet, a prestigious private residence commissioned by a wealthy textile manufacturer in the heart of Barcelona.

Like many of Gaudí's designs, the Calvet chair has a sculptural quality that epitomizes his highly individual, idiosyncratic version of Art Nouveau. It is raised on four elegant carved legs, with the rear pair splayed back almost sabre-style, and the front gently curved and terminating in his very individual interpretation of the traditional hoof foot. The seat and the back are ornately shaped and gently sculpted to embrace the human form: Gaudí was particularly concerned that his furniture should offer maximum support and comfort, and he studied the human form in detail to make sure that these criteria were met. Typically, however, he goes beyond supporting the spine into representing it as well. The carved support that connects the seat to the back not only cants the latter at a suitably supportive angle, but also looks like the skeletal base of a spine. Once this is spotted, one soon catches on that this is an anthropomorphic quality that pervades the rest of the design and indeed much of his work. Moreover, the chair is also typical of Gaudí's furniture in being made of solid oak – his wood of choice – and in its carved and pierced floral decoration – the latter rowed along the seat and set in a heart-shaped motif in the back.

Gaudí was one of a number of architect–designers around the turn of the 20th century who were commissioned to design not only buildings but also many of the features within them, including the furniture. Other names of note include Frank Lloyd Wright, Henry van de Velde, Charles Rennie Mackintosh (see pages 120 and 134) and Josef Hoffmann (see pages 136 and 142). For these men, the success of their work relied on the seamless integration of the interior design with that of the structural architecture. For the Casa Calvet, Gaudí designed a whole range of furniture to give the interior an homogenous look. Thus this side chair was also produced in armchair form and as a three-seater canapé, and a stool and a mirror were also made in the same style. Decorative flourishes, such as the carved and pierced detail on the back of the chair, were repeated throughout.

Today, original Calvet chairs are almost beyond price. Fortunately, in 1972 a group of Spanish designers founded a company operating today as Bd (Barcelona Design). Among their works are faithful reproductions of famous designs, and the Calvet chair is among them: armless as here, or armed, hand-carved from solid oak and constructed as it would have been under Gaudí's direction more than a century ago.

Above right
The floral organic and the skeletal anthropomorphic qualities of Gaudí's unique Calvet become even more evident when the chair is viewed from the back.

Hill House Ladderback / 1904

This exaggerated form of the traditional ladderback chair was the creation of the architect Charles Rennie Mackintosh (1868–1928) and was an integral part of his design for Hill House, the home he designed in 1902–4 for the publisher Walter Blackie in Helensburgh, Scotland. One of the most famous of all Mackintosh's pieces of furniture, the original chair continues to occupy the space for which it was designed, in a bedroom at Hill House. In fact, it was never intended for use as a chair, but as a decorative element within the scheme, for which Mackintosh designed most of the furnishings, from the wardrobes to the fire tongs.

The ladderback chair was and is essentially a vernacular form, instantly recognizable by the horizontal slats between the stiles or uprights of the chair's back. This basic configuration goes back many centuries, and is displayed in the late 18th-century Georgian country ladderback on page 68 and the Arts and Crafts ladderback on page 106. However, by extending the chair to 141cm (56in) in height, Mackintosh gave the form a very new, contemporary appeal. In his ladderback, the 'ladder' rises from floor level and stretches right up the back to about 25cm (10in) from the top, at which point a five-square grid completes the design. The narrow width of the back also makes the chair look even taller than it actually is, an effect that is further accentuated by the shape of the seat, which is gradually widened from back to front. Overall, the stark simplicity of the design, together with the absence of curves, is reminiscent of the Japanese influence that swept through much of Europe during the late 19th and early 20th century. Made from ash, the entire frame of the chair has an ebonized finish – a Western take on the Japanese black-lacquered furniture that Mackintosh so admired.

For many, Mackintosh bridged the gap between the Arts and Crafts and the Art Nouveau movements at the turn of the century. In contrast to the curvilinear style of Art Nouveau prevalent in France (see pages 124, 126 and 128). Mackintosh developed a unique, restrained and more rectilinear style of his own that became hugely influential in other parts of continental Europe, most notably in Austria among the designers of the Vienna Secession. Josef Hoffmann (see page 136), for example, avidly adopted Mackintosh's application of geometric forms. Indeed, it is because of developments such as this and a chair such as the Hill House ladderback that Mackintosh's work can be seen as foreshadowing the Modernist movement that began to really emerge in the 1920s.

FRAGILE
Please handle carefully
FURNITURE

Caberet Fledermaus / 1907

Like many visionaries, Josef Hoffmann (1870–1956) and his Wiener Werkstätte cohorts dreamed of creating a better world – a world where the middle classes would give up comfortable mediocrity for progressive, modern design. They aimed to liberate the stylistically challenged with their new architecture and furnishings, and in 1907 took the revolution to the theatre with the interiors of the Cabaret Fledermaus in Vienna.

Believing that there should be a unity between architecture, decoration and furnishings, Hoffmann and his Werkstätte colleagues created a *Gesamtkunstwerk*, or 'total work of art', at the Fledermaus. Everything, from the décor to the programme, from the publicity materials to the staff uniforms, was designed and made by members of the Werkstätte. Hoffmann's success was described by a critic at the time as 'wonderful – the proportions, the light atmosphere, cheerful flowing lines, elegant light fixtures, comfortable chairs of new shape and, finally, the whole tasteful ensemble. Genuine Hoffmann.'

Those comfortable chairs of new shape were designed for the cabaret's bar and provided a stylishly fitting contrast to its exuberant walls, which were covered with a mosaic of more than 7,000 vibrant ceramic tiles. Originally in white with black ball-shaped corner blocks, the chairs echoed the contrasts of a black-and-white tiled floor and were arranged around tables suitably covered with crisp white tablecloths. Innovative and elegantly simple, they not only acquired the name of their location, but also went on to become an icon of early 20th-century chair design.

Made by Thonet, the Cabaret Fledermaus chair features a distinctive horseshoe-shaped bentwood top rail that is echoed, rather than duplicated, in an elongated U-shaped stretcher. Both are fashioned from beech, as is the rest of the frame. Sited only just above floor height the stretcher unites four cylindrical legs that, in turn, support a bentwood seat frame with, in this case, an upholstered drop-in seat pad. Wooden seated versions have also been produced, in which instead of an upholstered back-pad they have a plain, curved wooden back-splat. Given their traditionally hidden functional role, the chairs supportive corner blocks – four under the seat, two under the top rail and all, unusually, ball-shaped – are wonderfully prominent geometric forms.

Typical of Hoffmann's chair designs, the Caberet Fledermaus was, despite that curved top rail and stretcher, the antithesis of the curvilinear French Art Nouveau style that was popular in Europe at the time. In fact, a major influence evident here and elsewhere in Hoffmann's work was the more rectilinear, geometric style of Art Nouveau pioneered by Charles Rennie Mackintosh. Stark, functional and progressive, the Cabaret Fledermaus chair has, however, an elegance that rescues it from appearing too austere. Indeed, it is a perfect realization of the Werkstätte's aim of designing simple, well-made furniture. Like its namesake Viennese cabaret – recently renovated and currently running as a nightclub – it has deservedly retained its desirability more than a century after conception.

Right above and below
Hoffmann's use of prominent corner blocks of unusual spherical form under the top and seat rails underpins the geometric qualities of his design.

American Arts & Crafts Armchair / c.1907–10

With its clean, plain geometric lines, this armchair by the American furniture maker Gustav Stickley (1857–1942) fulfils two of his mission statements: 'to teach that beauty does not imply elaboration or ornament' and 'to employ only those forms and materials which make for simplicity, individuality and dignity of effect'.

Born in Wisconsin, Stickley had initially acquired carpentry skills working in his uncle Jacob Schlager's, furniture factory. However, his design ethos was really formulated in the 1890s during a trip to Europe, where he met with some of the leading lights in the British Arts & Crafts movement and was captivated by their promotion of traditional methods of craftsmanship and their rejection of unnecessary, overwrought decoration.

On returning to the States, Stickley set up his own company in Eastwood, New York, in 1898, in order to produce household furniture, and in 1901 began publishing *Craftsman* magazine to promote both his furniture and his philosophy of design. From then until 1916, when he was forced to close the company in the face of competition and changing tastes in furniture styles, Stickley's designs enjoyed considerable success and became widely available across the United States. Collectively they are described as American Arts & Crafts, or Craftsman style (Stickley named his company The Craftsman Workshops from 1904), or Mission style – the latter because many pieces were said to have been inspired by the furniture found in the Spanish missions of colonial California.

Functional, sturdy, handsome and elegant, this armchair encapsulates the Stickley style. It is constructed from quarter-sawn oak – Stickley's material and cut of choice. Typically, its rich dark brown colour has been achieved by exposure to ammonia vapour rather than the application of wood stain – this fuming process also bringing out the decorative figuring of the quarter-sawn wood. Other than that, decoration subtly and characteristically resides in elements of the carpentry: in the pegged through-tenons at the ends of the stretchers, where they join the legs; in the arched corbels supporting the plank-cut arms; and in the vertical slats in the sides and back. On most of Stickley's early chairs, notably his Morris Chair No.332 which was an interpretation of an adjustable reclining armchair designed in England by Philip Webb for William Morris, these slats are much broader. Here, however, their slender more sophisticated forms establish a lighter, more vertical look that echo some of the furniture designs of Frank Lloyd Wright in the United States and Charles Rennie Mackintosh in Britain (see pages 120 and 134).

However, one significant difference between Stickley and many British Arts & Crafts designers lay in the fact that Stickley was prepared to use, to varying degrees, mechanical means of production, in contrast to the more 'purist', exclusively hand-crafted ethos on the other side of the Atlantic. But as this chair clearly reveals, techniques such as mechanized cutting were not in themselves a bar to high-quality construction. Moreover, they made it possible to manufacture such chairs in far great numbers and at significantly lower cost. Unlike most purely hand-crafted Arts & Crafts furniture, this made them admirably accessible to more than just a wealthy few.

Above
Exposed joints, in this case a pegged through-tenon joining a stretcher to a corner post, are a feature of Stickley's chairs and typical of the Arts & Crafts or Craftsman style.

Kubus / 1910

Geometry, in particular the square, is at the heart of many of the best-known designs of Josef Hoffmann (1870–1956), whether as windows, cutouts on a table leg, pierced decoration on a vase or a row of squares cut out along a chair back. When the designer renowned for linear patterns and well-defined vertical and horizontal lines turned his attention to an upholstered armchair, the result was squares again – but what a difference some padding and leather make. In Hoffmann's Kubus armchair, the proportions, legs and patchwork of leather are all based on the square or the cube. Originally unveiled at the Buenos Aires International Exhibition of 1910, it predates Le Corbusier's Gran Confort, another beacon of leather, comfort and Modernism, by some 18 years.

In a world obsessed at the time with the erotic curves of Art Nouveau or cocooned in the safety of historical revival styles, Hoffmann and his colleagues in the Wiener Werkstätte (a group he had helped to establish in 1903) promoted functional, modern design. Their aim was to rescue their wealthy patrons from what they considered to be the run-of-the-mill furnishings fashionable at the time by converting their homes into temples of geometric, functional, simple, well-executed modernity.

The Kubus has indeed a formal purity and simplicity. The quilted leather creates a smooth, well-defined surface that is both elegant and playful. Substantial, comfortable and still modern-looking today, it has stood the test of time. While it may appear to have been ahead of its time, the Kubus was also successful in its day – so much so that Hoffmann went on to design a two-seater loveseat and a three-seater sofa in the same style. All versions are traditionally upholstered in black leather, but grey, white, yellow and burgundy are also available.

Hoffmann was fascinated by the possibilities of the vertical and horizontal, and this obsession with geometry led his style to be nicknamed 'Quadratstil' (meaning 'square style'). There is a slightly perjorative quality to that description. It implies a rather dehumanized abstraction – until one realizes that what Hoffmann has succeeded in doing in the Kubus is to make geometry humanly tangible.

Above left
Kubus's overtly
geometric form
extends to cube legs
raised on ball feet.

Fischel Turned and Bentwood Armchair / c.1910–14

This chair was produced by the furniture manufacturer D G Fischel Söhne during the early years of the 20th century, not long before the outbreak of World War I. Its basic shape – an open armchair or carver – is not particularly original, and its methods of construction – turned and bentwood – are derivative, and yet it manages to work on all levels: aesthetic, physical and psychological.

In an opportunist, entrepreneurial move, the Fischel company had been founded by David Gabriel Fischel in 1870, just one month after Gebrüder Thonet's patent for manufacturing steamed and press-moulded bentwood furniture expired (see page 114). A vegetable-oil salesman from Prague, Fischel opened his factory at Niemes – then in Bohemia, now the Czech Republic – and put his son Alexander in charge. Having previously worked at Thonet's Koritschan factory, Alexander brought Thonet's manufacturing secrets with him, and soon Fischel Söhne had more than a hundred workers making more than a hundred bentwood chairs a day – most of which were nearly identical to Thonet's most popular models.

During the course of the 1870s to 1880s Fischel re-registered in Prague, expanded its workforce and output, and exhibited its products internationally, most notably at Barcelona's prestigious Universal Exposition of 1888. By the 1890s it was publishing catalogues illustrating chair designs incorporating not just bentwood, but also turned and carved components. By the time this chair was made, the company had been sold to Ernst Hirsch and its headquarters moved to Vienna.

Fashioned from beech, which was lacquered black to resemble the more fashionable ebony, the chair frame is raised on four turned legs. All are of slender, tapering circular section, but the rear pair is subtly bowed back below seat level to improve stability. This is further augmented with a bentwood stretcher uniting the legs and echoing the D-shaped seat above. Made of birch, the seat panel has an impressed concave centre to enhance the comfort and security of the occupant. Above the seat, a supportive Y-end back-splat rises to a one-piece top rail and arms. Cut, carved and bent to a D- or horseshoe shape, this is also raised on the tops of the legs, which serve as stiles at the back and as arm supports at the front.

Collectively, the result is a chair in which the proportions and posture are almost perfectly realized. Comfortable for deskwork, conversation and eating alike, it feels both physically and psychologically supportive, and looks it as well.

Red/Blue / 1917–23

As much a piece of abstract sculpture as a form of seating, the Red/Blue chair by the Dutch designer and architect Gerrit Rietveld (1888–1964) represents the moment that furniture design turned its back on some of the fundamental tenets of the Arts and Crafts movement and took a quantum leap towards Modernism. Indeed, the Modern movement's philosophy promoting designs without superfluous ornament for machine production is perfectly encapsulated in Rietveld's Red/Blue chair.

Rietveld designed the chair to be cheap to make and to buy – and, as he said, to prove it was possible to create something beautiful using machine-processed parts. Based on a relatively simple geometric construction, it has a framework consisting of 13 rails, set at right angles to each other, supporting the four boards that make up the seat, back and armrests. Rietveld had been an apprentice joiner, but he ignored much of his training and employed a series of overlapping dowelled joints, referred to as Cartesian nodes or Rietveld joints, to join and secure many of the component parts. The original version also incorporated side pieces enclosing the armrests, but Rietveld later omitted these.

Interestingly, the original chair was not painted in the primary colours now associated with it; instead, it had a natural wood finish, consistent with Rietveld's traditional training in cabinet-making. However, in 1919 he became associated with the De Stijl group of artists, and by 1923 he was painting the chair in the signature De Stijl colours – the back bright red, the seat blue and the supporting framework black with startlingly yellow ends. The result has been described as a '3-D Mondrian painting' – in reference to the Dutch painter Piet Mondrian (1872–1944), a leading member of De Stijl.

This movement – which took its name from the magazine De Stijl (The Style), launched in 1917 – aimed to achieve a universal style in painting, furniture and architecture, using rectangles in flat planes of primary colours and black and white. Rejecting naturalism and handcrafting, they sought clarity, order and a 'dynamic equilibrium' in design, which could be achieved through abstraction, geometry and machine production. Rietveld's radical designs for the Red/Blue fulfilled all these criteria and brought him to the attention of Mondrian and another of the movement's leaders, Theo van Doesburg. According to Doesburg, Rietveld's Red/Blue and other furniture had an 'unspeaking elegance like that of a machine' – the ultimate accolade.

In addition to its aesthetics, there is also the rather fundamental question of how comfortable is the chair? This of course depends on your definition of comfort. As Paul Overy in his book De Stijl points out: 'Rietveld was not interested in conventional ideas of comfort (the 19th century armchair that relaxes you so much that you spill your coffee or fall asleep over your book). He wished to keep the sitter physically and mentally toned up.' Thus, Overy continues, 'one of the functions of Rietveld's chairs, with their hard seats and backs, is to focus our senses, to make us alert and aware. Sit in a revolutionary Red/Blue, perhaps contemplate space, colour and form, and you will soon realise Rietveld certainly achieved his goal.

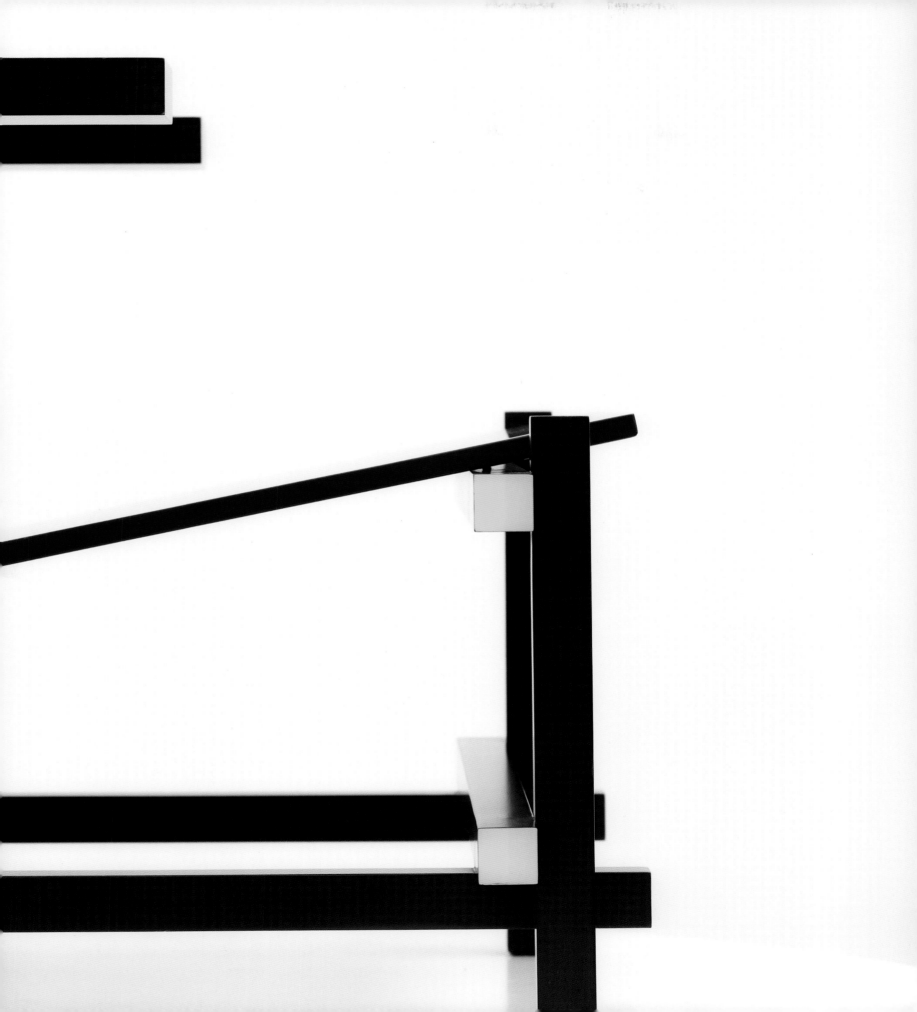

French Art Deco Armchair / 1920s

The specific provenance of this chair is uncertain. However, it is definitely French, and fashioned in the Art Deco style of the mid-1920s. A relatively modern attribution the term 'Art Deco' was coined in the 1960s to describe retrospectively and collectively the architecture and artefacts on display at the Exposition Internationale des Arts Décoratifs et Industriels Modernes held in Paris in 1925. Eminent and influential French designers who created chairs in this style include Paul Follot, Jules Leleu, Maurice Dufrène and Pierre Chareau. Although probably not by one of them, the chair is nevertheless likely to have been inspired by numerous aspects of their work, and would have been a sophisticated and highly fashionable purchase at the time of its manufacture.

The chair also gives the lie to a popular misconception about Art Deco. It is true that many designers working under the aegis of the Art Deco movement drew for inspiration on Cubism, Aztec imagery, and motifs suggesting speed, dynamism and streamlining symbolic of the machine age; however, the stepped shapes and angular geometric forms this resulted in are to be found on many Art Deco chairs from c.1929 onwards. As this chair demonstrates, they are not characteristic of Art Deco designs of the mid-1920s. Indeed, the basic inspiration for the form of this chair lies in the pre-industrial 18th century, rather than the industrial 20th century.

More specifically, the shape of the seat, sides and back of the chair evoke the sweeping graceful curves of a late 18th-century Louis XVI *bergère* – a close English equivalent being a George III *bergère*-like tub chair (see page 70). Moreover, as with many of its luxurious 18th-century forebears, the Art Deco chair characteristically incorporates expensive and rather exotic-looking materials – in this case finely figured rosewood veneer for the exposed sections of the frame, as well as for the legs.

But, this chair is no mere copy of an 18th-century prototype. That later Art Deco angularity is just beginning to surface and is evident in the three-sided profile of the upholstered seat front and underlying chair rail, and also in the front legs. These are in the form of arm-high posts, of slender square section and tapering to block feet of faux ivory. The latter, together with the smooth leather upholstery and the seamless integration of the angular and the curvaceous elements, transforms 18th-century elegance into 1920s Art Deco opulence.

Above right
While the hidden elements of the chair frame are made of beech, the exposed areas and legs are veneered with expensive and finely figured rosewood.

B3 (Wassily) / 1925

Said to have been inspired by the curved metal handlebars on his bicycle, Marcel Breuer's first tubular steel chair is an exciting contrast of hard metal and pliable leather. But its generous width – reminiscent of an English club chair – gives it a sense of comfort few will find perched on a narrow bicycle seat.

The B3, later renamed the Wassily, is probably the most copied of all the chairs designed by the Hungarian architect and designer Breuer (1902–81). It was among the first pieces of furniture constructed from tubular steel when it was designed in 1925. The chair's overlapping planes were inspired by the early chair designs of Gerrit Rietveld, but show the design possibilities of the revolutionary new material.

The B3's apparent simplicity belies its clever construction. Nine pieces of metal tube are screwed together to give the appearance of a single, continuous length and create a framework that supports the weight of the sitter. The seat, back and armrests originally consisted of five fabric slings, but later versions substituted thick leather. The result is comfortable, sturdy yet lightweight, and visually far from substantial – and thanks to the screws the chair is simple to dismantle and rebuild should the need or desire arise. It is also worth noting that, while early versions of the chair were nickel-plated, the majority of examples are chrome-plated.

Breuer was a student and later a teacher at the Bauhaus, and the chair was used in the school buildings from 1926. It was later renamed the Wassily because Breuer made a duplicate of the chair for the abstract painter Wassily Kandinsky, who was teaching at the Bauhaus at the time and had admired the design. Breuer said of the chair, 'I thought that this out of all my work would earn me the most criticism, but the opposite of what I expected came true.'

The B3 was emblematic of the Bauhaus designers' declared aim of breaking down the barriers between art, craft, design and architecture. It helped to make metal furniture acceptable not just in commercial and institutional settings, but also in domestic interiors. There was, however, resistance from consumers to buying tubular-steel furniture because it was more expensive than wood. Until the price fell in the late 1930s, it was mostly bought by an affluent elite.

Today the chair, which delighted some of the greatest designers and artists of the 1920s, may seem ubiquitous in loft apartments and office blocks around the world – but if that is the case, then the B3 is a fitting legacy for a furniture pioneer.

Right
The slenderness of the steel tubing and the openess of the design belie the strength of the Wassily's frame.

B33 / 1926–7

The development of the first successful cantilever chair was the Holy Grail of design for Modernist designers. A chair in which the sitter appeared to float in mid-air, which had two legs rather than four, and on which the weight of the sitter was supported by a single point on the frame was every 1920s designer's dream. But who first created this landmark design?

The Dutch architect Mart Stam, the German architect Ludwig Mies van der Rohe and the Hungarian architect Marcel Breuer all experimented with bending tubular steel to create furniture during the 1920s, and these trials included the cantilever chairs that they all exhibited in 1927. Stam and Mies van der Rohe showed their designs in public first at the Die Wohnung exhibition in Stuttgart, but it was Breuer (1902–81) who, despite not exhibiting his design until later that year, went on to exploit the form with the B33. His chair had the better proportions and, as it was made from tubular steel that had not been reinforced, was more hard-wearing and comfortable than other models.

Sitting in such an unconventional chair for the first time – your body suspended over the base and relying on just two 'legs' for support – remains as surprising now as it was then. The B33 is the type of pure form that Modernist designers craved: a single length of tubular steel bent into shape to create a stable frame, then fitted with a wood, cane or canvas seat and back. The result is comfortable, practical, easy to mass-produce and utterly simple. Breuer enhanced the design by adding steel rods under the seat for stability, curving them so that they were not felt by the person sitting in the chair. The rail at the top of the chair back extends outwards, allowing the chair to be pushed under a table, and pulled away from it, effortlessly. The seat and back are substantial enough to offer good support, but remain comfortable. Other examples have slightly bowed runners at the base to prevent them rocking on uneven floors.

Breuer saw his task as that of 'civilizing technology'. The development of these new models helped to do this and created a revolution in furniture design. Such was the success of the B33 that he went on to design variations such as the B34 (which featured armrests), a folding chair and various tables. It continues to inspire countless copies.

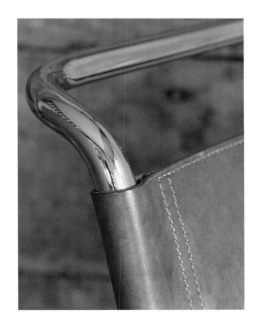

Above
Ergonomic perfection includes a curved back rail that allows the chair to be effortlessly pushed under or pulled out from a table.

MR10 & MR20 / 1927

In the summer of 1927, the city of Stuttgart hosted a ground-breaking showcase of architecture, the Weissenhof Siedlung Exhibition. Ludwig Mies van der Rohe (1886–1969) was in charge of the project, the brief for which was to produce a cohesive development in the International architectural style, comprising 60 dwellings in 21 buildings designed by a selection of Europe's most progressive architects, including Le Corbusier, Walter Gropius and Mart Stam. The entire estate was erected in just five months using prefabricated elements and – perhaps surprisingly given the number of architects – did have an overall visual cohesion. Mies had championed what he termed 'skin and bones' architecture – a 'less is more' concept that he also applied to his furniture designs and, specifically, the MR10 and MR20 chairs he designed for his block of 24 apartments.

Following on from Mart Stam's S33 cantilever design of 1926, Mies created something far more refined in the armless MR10 (shown right). Stam's chair had certain structural failings, most notably the fact that the acute right-angled tubular frame was prone to collapse unless it was internally reinforced. Mies addressed this problem by using a wide sweeping arc, which not only gave the chair much greater resilience and strength, but also made it more aesthetically pleasing. In conjunction with the ethos of his interiors, the chair was simple and light, just like the movable walls of his Weissenhof apartments.

With the addition of long, flowing arms, its equally refined sister chair, the MR20 (shown overleaf), is in some respects reminiscent of the mid-19th-century wrought-iron rocking chairs produced by R. W. Winfield and exhibited at the Great Exhibition of 1851 – and yet, like its sister, its form is somehow exclusively and exquisitely Mies van der Rohe. The 'fluid' minimal framework of both chairs was produced in nickel, chromium plate or various coloured lacquer finishes, and their 'less is more' qualities were extended to the upholstery: with woven cane Eisengard fabric (a tough weave designed by the Bauhaus Dessau to retain its shape) or hide seats, Mies again achieved optimum comfort with minimal fuss.

Just as Mies's architectural legacy is still with us in so many ways, so are the chairs that were modelled in the ethos of that legacy and accompanied its birth. Manufactured by Knoll in a number of variants, both chairs are still much in demand and, like two of their Mies van der Rohe stablemates – the Barcelona and the Brno (see pages 173 and 176) – the MR10 and the MR20 have become icons of 20th-century design.

Above left
The curved configuration of the MR10's tubular steel frames lends the chair considerable resilience and strength. The MR20 (overleaf) has the same frame, albeit with the addition of arms.

Chaise Longue No. B306 / 1928

As the father of Modern architecture, and one of the most influential architects in history, Le Corbusier has godlike stature in the world of design. His chaise longue B306 has similar status, but its design is not attributable to Le Corbusier alone.

Born in Switzerland, Charles-Edouard Jeanneret-Gris (1887–1965) adopted the pseudonym Le Corbusier in 1920 – a fashionable artistic conceit in France at that time, especially in Paris where he was working. Two years later, with his cousin Pierre Jeanneret (1896–1967), he established in the French capital a design studio – into which, in 1927, walked 24-year-old Charlotte Perriand (1903–99). Le Corbusier's blunt rejection of her request to join the studio as a furniture designer – 'we don't embroider cushions here' – was reversed, with an apology, months later when Pierre Jeanneret took him to see the glass, steel and aluminium rooftop bar Perriand had designed for the Salon d'Automne exhibition of that year. Their resulting collaboration did no less than usher in the machine-age aesthetic to domestic interiors and produced some of the most seminal works in design history – the Chaise Longue B306 being one of the best known.

Underpinning Le Corbusier's designs was a desire to provide a better lifestyle for the less advantaged sections of society. In theory, this meant that his furniture designs should be mass-produced and hence more affordable. In practice, however, manufacturing complications meant they were expensive. A political and social disappointment certainly, but not an artistic one.

Exhibited at the 1929 Salon d'Automne as part of a group of 'systemized' furniture entitled *l'équipement de l'habitation* (home equipment), the B306 displayed a purity of form and line that encapsulated the Purist movement's ideal – as advocated by Le Corbusier – of perfect geometric forms inspired by modern machinery. To describe the B306 as 'pure' seems almost an understatement. Its rational supine design is so resolutely resolved that to lie on it makes you as one with it. Moreover, the exposure of the tubular-steel framework is a highly functional and artistic statement that in no way undermines the comfort of the web-supported cushions on what Le Corbusier nicknamed the 'relaxing machine'.

The B306 was originally manufactured by Thonet. Nowadays, there are numerous copies on the market, but Cassina is the only officially licensed manufacturer of Le Corbusier's designs, having acquired the rights in 1964, while he was still alive. The chaise is currently manufactured in matt black or chromed tubular steel, with a matt black iron base; despite the enduring popularity of bovine leather and pony-skin covers, an original canvas version is also available. In Le Corbusier's own words, 'Long live the good taste manifested by choice, subtlety, proportion and harmony.'

Grand Confort LC2 / 1928

When in 1927 a 24-year-old Charlotte Perriand (1903–99) joined the Parisian design practice that Le Corbusier (1887–1965) and his cousin Pierre Jeanneret (1896–1967) had established in Paris, she had already read Le Corbusier's 1925 treatise on architecture and design, *L'Art décoratif d'aujourd'hui* (Decorative Art of Today). Perriand's enthusiastic adoption of his Purist preference for perfectly rationalized geometric forms, combined with her cutting-edge experiments in mechanical fabrication and hitherto unconventional combinations of materials – notably glass, steel, aluminium and leather – was to usher in the machine-age aesthetic.

The best-known product of this hugely influential collaboration was the chaise longue B306 (see page 162), but equally innovative was the armchair known as the Grand Confort LC2. Like the famous chaise longue, it was part of an architectural commission, but in this case a pair of semidetached houses in Paris known as the Villa Jeanneret–La Roche. Prior to Perriand's arrival at the design practice, the furniture store Maples of London had supplied club chairs for a number of Le Corbusier's projects, and the Grand Confort LC2 does indeed bear a clear resemblance to the boxy-looking gentleman's club chairs of the 1920s. There is, however, one important difference: the LC2 wears its bones on the outside, in the form of a chromium exoskeleton that wonderfully mirrors the ocean-liner look of Le Corbusier's architecture and the machine-age aesthetic.

This maritime quality is no coincidence. One only has to look at Le Corbusier's Villa Savoye to see how its rooftop garden echoes the walkways of those transatlantic leviathans. The LC2 – named entirely appropriately Grand Confort – is unashamedly luxurious in the same vein. In complying with the structural and ideological elements of Le Corbusier's design manifesto, it is quite simply a perfect 'vision of deluxe modernity'. This should not be surprising. As Perriand once said, 'We work with ideals.'

Designed in 1928 and exhibited in Paris at the 1929 Salon d'Automne as part of the *l'équipement de l'habitation* (home equipment) group, the LC2 was originally manufactured by Thonet. Since 1965 Cassina has been the officially licensed manufacturer. It is available as an armchair or as a two- or three-seater sofa (LC3), while the tubular exoskeleton is produced in chromed steel or various enamelled colours. With loose cushions available in woven fabric or leather, again in a range of shades, the Grand Confort LC2 remains enduringly popular and, in many respects, a perfect epithet for the ever-glamorous International Style.

Above right
The LC2 wears its bones on the outside, in the form of a tubular steel exoskeleton either chromed, as here, or enamelled in various colours, including basalt, grey, light blue, green, bordeaux and ochre.

Bibendum / 1929

The giveaway clue to what inspired the voluptuous, inviting design by Eileen Gray (1879–1976) for the Bibendum chair lies in the name. Bibendum, also known as the Michelin Man, is one of the world's oldest trademarks, and his rotund form has been used to sell tyres for more than a century. Gray wanted to create a design that spoke not only of comforts, but also of contemporaneity. Considering that the car industry was very glamorous at the time, one can see why Gray (who was largely involved with designing interiors for high-society Parisian clients) settled on the image of the tyre to inspire her design.

In reality, the industrial edge that the design carries (with a simple chromed tubular steel base and elementary forms) was somewhat tokenistic. The chair was intended only for one-off handmade production (specifically, for the apartment of one Madame Mathieu-Lévy), and went into wider production only some 50 years after it was first designed.

While clearly enamoured of the industrial aesthetic championed by the Modern Movement (and its cutting-edge connotations), Gray was little interested in the accompanying ideology. Her early designs leaned strongly towards Art Deco, and even in later life she never lost her love of this more frivolous style. Although many Modern Movement designers were involved in cutting their designs to the bone, it is typical of Gray that her Bibendum chair retains an unabashed plumpness.

As a rare female voice in the overtly male world of furniture design at the time, Gray was used to going against the grain. The fact that she pursued a less clearly defined path, however, than many of her male contemporaries (and that she felt little need to shout about her achievements in the design publications of the age) meant that her work was largely overlooked until the late 1970s.

It was then that the London-based furniture manufacturer Zeev Aram bought the rights to Gray's designs. Particularly taken by a single, grainy photo of the Bibendum chair in Madame Mathieu-Lévy's apartment, he decided to put the chair into production. Aram consulted the ailing memory of an ageing Gray for details of the design and construction, and also placed newspaper ads appealing for any further photographs or, indeed, original chairs.

In this way the chair was relaunched and went on to become a defining element of the 1980s style culture. In his 1985 book *Cult Objects*, the design critic Deyan Sudjic wrote, 'If you really want to lay claims to be regarded as a person of taste and discrimination, this is the chair to have casually placed about the place.'

MR90 (Barcelona) / 1929

In 1929, two years after designing the MR10 and MR20 chairs (see page 158) and a year before he was appointed the last director of the Bauhaus, the German-born architect Ludwig Mies van der Rohe (1886–1969) designed the MR90. Undoubtedly one of the brightest stars in the firmament of seating, this was to become the chair that launched a thousand copies! In fact, Mies didn't design it on his own, but in collaboration with his companion and working partner at the Deutscher Werkbund, Lilly Reich. It was conceived as part of a much larger commission, the design of the Barcelona Pavilion. This was Germany's pavilion at the 1929 International Exhibition in Barcelona – hence the chair's more commonly used epithet, the Barcelona.

Intended as a serious design statement, the Barcelona Pavilion was a stunningly beautiful building, unabashed in its opulent use of travertine and marble. The MR90 was equally stunning – a true icon of Modernism and befitting the seating intended for the King of Spain Alfonso XIII and his queen when they visited the pavilion. Although the original pavilion was demolished in 1930 after the exhibition closed, it was rebuilt in 1986, and this has provided the opportunity to view once again the MR90 in its original context. It clearly thrives in a light, spacious and grand environment, which is not surprising: its X-frame design has its origins in some of the most ancient and eminent seating – the senators' and magistrates' *sella curulis* of republican and Imperial Rome, and the *diphros okladias* of Classical Greece. Moreover, both of these were developments of the even older, folding X-frame stools used by royalty in ancient Egypt.

Of course, Mies' and Reich's Modernist take on these venerable prototypes was to forge the MR90's X-frame from chromed flat steel. Originally, the frame was bolted together, but from 1950 it was reconfigured with 'seamless' welded joints, a change that enhanced the inherent fluidity of its form. Manufactured by Knoll since 1953, under exclusive rights accorded to them by Mies, it is today produced in high-quality chromed stainless steel, expensively hand-buffed to a mirror finish. Supported by leather straps, the removable seat and back cushions are nowadays foam-filled and covered in hand-welted and deep-buttoned bovine leather (in lieu of the original pigskin). Classic colours for the leather are black, white and tan, although diverse other hues – as this example illustrates – have also become available.

It is a poignant thought that Lilly Reich never saw the MR90 put into commercial production. Immensely successful, it continues to exude style and luxury, while combining the gravitas of prestigious historical precedent with all the élan of Modernism.

Above
Supported by thick leather straps, the back and seat cushions conform to the sweeping curves of the polished-chromed steel frame.

MR50 (Brno) / 1929–30

As a cantilever chair the MR50 was by no means a new idea. Designed by the German architect Ludwig Mies van der Rohe (1886–1969), in collaboration with the German designer Lilly Reich (1885–1947), it was openly influenced by the earlier, cantilevered tubular-steel chairs by the Dutch architect Mart Stam (his S33 of 1926) and by the Hungarian-born architect Marcel Breuer (in particular his B33 of 1927 – see page 156). However, like Mies van der Rohe and Reich's iconic MR90 (Barcelona) chair (see page 172), the MR50 was designed for a specific space. Over and above that, it was part of something much bigger: a Modernist concept – a design for life.

The specific space in question was the Tugendhat Villa in Brno, Czechoslovakia (now the Czech Republic), and it was the Brno location that provided the name by which the MR50 is better known. Commissioned from Mies by Fritz and Greta Tugendhat, the villa, now a UNESCO World Heritage Site, was a masterpiece of Modernist design, similar in many ways to Mies's German pavilion at the 1929 International Exhibition in Barcelona. Like the other chair, the MR70 (dubbed the Tugendhat chair), that Mies and Reich designed for the villa, the MR50 is an integral part of the building: if you were told it had grown out of the floor, you would not question it. The structure of the villa is radical – its steel frame allowed for fewer internal partitions and the use of large expanses of glass. The MR50 is similarly 'uncluttered' and has 'space' built in to it: the flat-bar chromed-steel construction of the frame pares it down to a simple yet sophisticated form, making it less obtrusive within its environment, but conversely more imposing in its design.

This elegant simplicity extends to the upholstered seat and back rest. Virtually square and relatively slender, they perfectly complement the aesthetics of the frame. Of equal importance, however, is the fact that they are supportive and comfortable – qualities enhanced by just the right amount of 'give' in the cantilevered frame when the chair is in use. In these respects, the MR50 strikes a beautiful balance between form and function, design and use.

Still very much in production, the MR50 is offered by the manufacturer Knoll in more than 100 woven fabrics, 18 different types and qualities of leather, and more than 500 colours. In addition, there is the option of matching armpads and the choice of a polished stainless-steel or a polished mirror-chrome finish to the frame. Knoll also produces a version with a tubular-steel frame (a variant Mies and Reich had originally considered); although this version is a fluid and streamlined design, its profile is somehow less pleasing, and certainly less unique, than that of the truly iconic flat-bar MR50 original.

Above
To bear the considerable load imposed on a cantilevered frame, the original MR50 utilizes thick flat-bar steel (polished or chromed), although a bent tubular-steel version is also available.

Lloyd Loom (No. 60) / c.1930

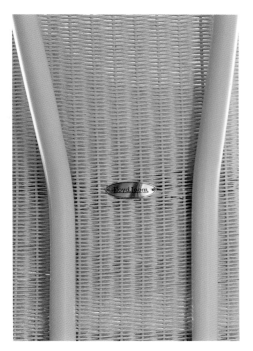

As quintessentially British as afternoon tea on the lawn or a game of cricket, the Lloyd Loom chair has seen service in the Royal Box at Wimbledon and for many years was standard issue for the British Army and Royal Air Force all over the world. Many a Battle of Britain pilot sat in a Lloyd Loom chair waiting for the call to take to the skies.

Despite its British associations, the story behind the Lloyd Loom chair begins thousands of miles away, in Menominee, Michigan. There, a prolific inventor called Marshall Burns Lloyd (1858–1927) was determined to find a cost-effective substitute for hand-woven wicker, to use in manufacturing baby carriages. Lloyd had worked as a soap pedlar, rural postman, land speculator, farmer and shoe salesman while developing the machines and processes that would eventually make him a multimillionaire. In 1907 he succeeded in creating a new woven fibre, made from twisted kraft paper reinforced with steel wire. Woven on a special loom, then bound to a wooden frame, it was 30 times faster to produce than hand-woven wicker. Lloyd named it Lloyd Loom Weave and patented it ten years later.

Commercial exploitation of his invention made Lloyd the largest producer of baby carriages in the world. Most of his competitors bought licences to use his looms, and in 1922 the American 'Baby Carriage King' sold the British patent to a salvage merchant, William Lusty, and his son Frank. They set up the W Lusty Lloyd Loom Co. Ltd to manufacture furniture, and an iconic English brand was born. In fact, Marshall Lloyd was diversifying into Lloyd Loom furniture at the same time in the United States, but it never achieved the same popularity there as in Britain.

In its heyday, prior to World War II, Lusty had a catalogue of more than 400 Lloyd Loom products. Today the range is smaller – approximately 25 different chairs, two stools, four settees, six tables, and four storage boxes, available in a limited but well-chosen range of colours. Yet demand is still considerable. Part of that can be explained by the fact that the Lloyd Loom 'paper wicker' is not only harder wearing than wicker or rattan, but also softer and more comfortable to sit on. Its smooth, uniform weave is also less likely to scratch skin or snag clothing. However, as this example – Model No.60 designed c.1930 by Jim Lusty – ably demonstrates, their enduring appeal ultimately resides in style and comfort. Supported on a sturdy bentwood frame, the No.60's sweeping arched back and out-splayed arms always invite a would-be occupant to relax into its generously proportioned seat. Contributing to the symmetry and elegance of the design, the front and side aprons below the seat also, somehow, enhance that feeling of security one invariably feels sitting – or indeed catnapping – in a classic Lloyd Loom.

Right top
Fashioned from twisted kraft paper reinforced with steel wire, the Lloyd Loom Weave is formed over a bentwood frame of circular section.

Right below
The outer edges of the one-piece top rail and arms, and the front of the arm supports, are traditionally finished with a braided paper trim.

Paimio No. 31 / 1931–2

In the early 1930s the architect Alvar Aalto (1898–1976) designed a tuberculosis sanatorium at Paimio, in his native Finland. The two chairs he designed specifically for the project – the No. 41 and, shown here, the No. 31 – were the product of more than five years' ground-breaking research into bending and moulding laminated woods and plywood. Initially conducted by Aalto and his wife, Aino Marsio, and later also with craftsman–carpenter Otto Korhonen, these experiments were to prove as revolutionary for chair design as Michael Thonet's development of steamed and press-moulded solid wood – bentwood – a century earlier (see page 114).

Although Aalto's chair designs were strongly influenced by the forms of the German and Dutch Modernists' tubular steel chairs of the 1920s (see pages 154 and 156), his use of wood was, at the beginning of the 1930s, distinctly un-Modernist. Aalto explained that this was because he found their machine-age steel designs lacking in 'human qualities'. Mies van der Rohe, however, attributed Aalto's preference for the medium of wood simply to the fact that he lived 'deep in a forest'. Of course, these two explanations are not incompatible, and either way there is no doubt that Aalto's use of wood helped to 'humanize' Modernism – a development that was to inspire Gerald Summers's designs in Britain.

The way in which Aalto used wood was essentially the same in the No. 41 and No. 31 chairs. Their combination arms and legs are moulded to shape in laminated birch wood, while the undulating seat/back is moulded in thinner birch ply, then lacquered. Here the lacquer is black, but clear, white or various colours are now also available from the manufacturer, Artek.

There are, however, a couple of differences between the two Paimio chairs. The No. 41's seat/back is looped extravagantly rather than curved at either end, and its combined arms and legs form, on each side, a fully enclosed rectangle, which undulates inwardly where it falls level with the front of the seat. In contrast, the No. 31's combined arms and legs are of a curving, open-ended form that made it the first chair in the world successfully to employ laminated wood in a cantilevered structure – a development made possible by the 'man-made' strength of laminated layers of birch, but also aided by the inherent springiness of this particular wood.

While the technical achievements of the No. 31 and the No. 41 are impressive, they are by no means their only virtue. In addition to humanizing Modernism, they also put Scandinavian design on the map, and in so doing paved the way for the plethora of great Scandinavian chair designers that followed during the course of the 20th century. Perhaps most impressive of all, however, is the fact that, given that the No. 31 and No. 41 were originally designed for occupants with serious respiratory problems, the angle formed by the seat and back actually facilitates a posture that makes it easier to breathe.

Above
Tenoned into a cantilevered frame of clear-lacquered laminated birch, the bent birch ply seat of this Paimio No. 31 has a black lacquer finish.

Bent Plywood Armchair / 1933–4

Although the English designer Gerald Summers (1899–1967) had experimented with bent plywood furniture construction since the late 1920s, significant inspiration for his now-iconic armchair was provided by the chairs Alvar Aalto had designed c.1931 for the Paimio sanatorium in Finland (see page 180). Critical acclaim for an exhibition of Aalto's chairs at the Fortnum & Mason department store in London in 1933 had intimated that, when it came to streamlined Modernist designs, warmer, more organic bent plywood might be better suited to British tastes than cold, overtly industrial tubular steel. This was a sentiment with which Summers concurred. The result, however, was no mere copy of Aalto's work.

While Aalto had hung an undulating birch plywood seat and back between combined arms and legs of solid bentwood birch, Summers took the overall form of the design to its logical conclusion. His chair dispensed with joints or connectors, and its combined arms, legs, feet, seat and back were cut and bent in different directions from a single sheet of birch plywood. In using just one material and therefore dispensing with the labour costs of assembly, Summers achieved one of the holy grails of industrial design, and pre-empted by almost three decades one-piece chair construction with moulded plastics. The chair also had the virtue of being comfortable, even without cushions. In addition, it was promoted as being ideal for use in tropical climates – its smooth surfaces and the absence of traditional joints, and of upholstery, made it theoretically less vulnerable to insect infestation and extremes of humidity.

Summers's own company, Makers of Simple Furniture Ltd, produced the chair from 1934 until the firm's closure in 1939 following wartime government restrictions on the importation and use of plywood. During that short period only 120 chairs were made – which begs the question, why the relative lack of commercial success? This can be partly attributed to the fact that the back legs could break if overloaded and partly to Summers's lack of marketing and publicity skills. Ultimately, however, the chair was outsold by its Scandinavian rivals because they were less expensive.

Seventy years on, Summers's armchair is back in production with the Italian company Alivar, while 1930s originals command considerable prices when they appear on the market. Such desirability essentially resides in an appreciation of the ingenuity of the unified form, which is simultaneously simple and clever. A concise, fluent composition of streamlined curves, with both abstract and biomorphic qualities, Summers's armchair displays an economical elegance that ensures its status as a classic of Modernist design.

Above left
Smooth, streamlined curves are ingeniously cut and bent from a single sheet of birch plywood.

Eva / 1934

'Eternally young, bold and elegant' – fitting words indeed for a classic design. The Eva chair echoes all of these in ample measure, yet all were words used to describe the chair's designer, Bruno Mathsson (1907–88). However, he was also called 'wilful, stubborn and clever', and perhaps all of these characteristics were necessary ingredients in his designs.

Mathsson's father was a fifth-generation master cabinet-maker, and the young Bruno learned his trade in his father's workshop in Värnamo, Sweden. The traditional skills and understanding of wood that he acquired were of unparalleled importance to his development. He began exploring the possibilities of bent laminated wood, and in 1931 he produced the elegant Grasshopper chair with a bent laminated beech frame and woven linen seat. It was not an immediate success but, like many future classics, it rode on the back of Mathsson's subsequent success with the Eva chair, proving to be an important precursor and recognizable milestone in his career.

The Eva chair was developed in 1934. The frame, constructed of bent laminated birch with natural hemp webbing, differed a little from the more familiar, refined model of 1941 (pictured here), but the strength and elegance of the construction with minimalist details make the Eva a classic design. This refined version uses a mixture of carved and laminated birch in its construction, with the signature webbed hemp seat.

Detractors have argued that the Eva chair has similarities to Alvar Aalto's designs but, like many a great designer, Mathsson arrived at his concepts through an unusual understanding of his materials and surroundings. He aimed for a versatility in his chairs that would allow them to adapt to their environment – the Eva, for example, could be either a lounge chair or an office chair – and to the occupant's body. He was convinced that people would think and work more efficiently 'in positions of repose'. Mathsson's approach was unconventional; he challenged traditional values and adapted his furniture for lower surfaces. His concept of 'ultimate sitting' is definitively illustrated in the ergonomic principles enshrined in the Eva's design and the fact that its curved shape and built-in elasticity make it luxuriously comfortable yet understated. Like many of his designs, it has a woman's name – perhaps a hint at the sensuousness of its form.

Bruno Mathsson's accolades are numerous and his legacy is enduring, with designs such as the Eva continually in production and currently manufactured by Dux. Even today his work looks no less modern than many contemporary pieces – a fitting comment for a world-class designer whose innovative furniture is exhibited in museums and enjoyed in homes and workplaces all round the globe.

Above right
Like the rest of the frame to which they are bolted, Eva's arms are moulded from laminated birch wood, while her upholstery is woven from hemp webbing.

Standard / 1934

Jean Prouvé once said that he liked his furniture designs to express 'what the material thinks'. In the case of his Standard chair, the use of bulky hindquarters with slim front legs states that, as with most chairs, it is the rear two legs that take the most strain when someone sits down. This visual portrayal of the load-bearing qualities of a chair has the effect of giving the Standard a voice, raising its status from a meek, mute object to a proud and trusty servant.

Jean Prouvé was a man with strong egalitarian beliefs. Despite a successful career, he was never tempted to leave his hometown of Nancy, France (where he was mayor for a time), for the brighter lights of Paris. As a designer he was more at home producing pieces for schools, town halls and even petrol stations than he was for private clients or upmarket boutiques.

His designs, as exemplified by the Standard chair, have a rugged yet lyrical charm, almost despite themselves. Indeed, this combination of Prouvé's graceful, almost feminine feeling for form with his more macho approach to construction and choice of materials accounts for much of the appeal of his work.

The Standard chair is sometimes referred to as 'Chair No. 4', as it was his fourth attempt at creating a versatile office chair. Of course, now that offices are routinely equipped with swivel chairs, the Standard more often takes up residence in restaurants, cafés and homes. It must be pointed out that the chair often now finds itself in relatively refined surroundings, having been adopted by an educated, usually wealthy, design-literate elite since it was put into production again in 2002 by Vitra. (Ateliers Jean Prouvé, his manufacturing company, had stopped producing the chair in 1956.) Whether Prouvé himself would be pleased or appalled by this new fan base we shall never know.

One of the most endearing aspects of the Standard chair, to contemporary consumers, is that, although it speaks the language of standardized industrial production, this is clearly a chair created by one man in a workshop, not on an office computer. Prouvé was known to prefer designing with materials and tools in front of him, as opposed to sitting at a drawing desk. Having started his career as a blacksmith, he never lost his love for getting his hands dirty. This is why the design for the Standard chair was continually being tinkered with over the 22 years that Ateliers Jean Prouvé produced it. Indeed, it was some years after it was first conceived that Prouvé altered the design to allow the chair to be easily dismantled for storage and transportation.

Above left
The steel frame has a powder-coated finish available in blue, green, aubergine (eggplant), black, shades of red and, as here, yellow.

Left
The varnished oak seat and back rest are screwed to the frame with chromed bolts.

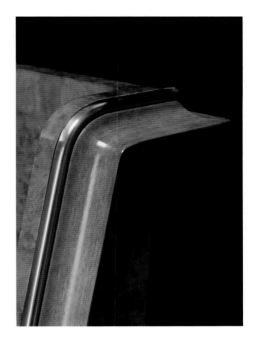

Art Moderne 'Day-bed' / c.1935

What on earth is a bed, albeit a day bed, doing in a book on chairs? It is included because, regardless of its maker's classification or its location in a house or apartment – in the boudoir or in the salon – the use to which it would often have been originally put differed little from that of a chaise longue. In well-to-do households, the latter has an impressive lineage running back through the Victorian chaise longue (see page 102), via its Regency forebear (see page 84), to the couch-like *lectus* of Imperial Rome. Although employed for daytime napping, it was more extensively used as a reclining seat for informal relaxing and entertaining.

There is, of course, a second and more important justification for the day bed's inclusion: in its form and style, in the quality of its construction and the materials used, and in the provenance of its designer, it is a simply superb example of mid- to late 1930s Art Moderne furniture. The designer was Etienne Kohlmann (1903–88), whose credentials include work for the influential Parisian department store Grands Magasins du Louvre in the early 1930s and for the Pavilion d'Elégance at the Paris International Exhibition of 1937.

Above all, Kohlmann designed with luxury in mind, and that is clearly evident here. Constructed from beech, the base and the headboard of the day bed are veneered with burr walnut, the warm yellowish-brown tones and variegated dramatic figuring of which instantly convey 1930s opulence. The sense of the latter is also significantly enhanced by the use of gold-like decorative brass mounts, which complement the original satin-silk cover of the cushion and bolster. (Although already matching when uncovered, the original mattress would have been similarly draped when in use.)

Inevitably with Kohlmann's designs, the brass mounts do far more than contribute to colour and pattern – they also help to define the day bed's most impressive quality: its shape. The 1930s was an era in which success and luxury were to a considerable extent defined by speed and travel, and nothing better represented these than the fast, luxuriously appointed ocean liners such as *L'Atlantique* and, most notably, the *SS Normandie* (whose maiden voyage was in 1935). Their elegant forms are echoed here in the day bed's elongated shape, which becomes particularly evident when viewed in profile (see page 192). Just like the exteriors of many houses and apartments built or refaced during the mid- to late 1930s, this streamlined nautical look represented the ultimate in luxurious Modernity.

Right above and below
The superb quality of the day bed is evident in the high standards of cabinet-making and the use of finely figured burr walnut veneers offset with brass mounts.

Pelikan / 1940

The Pelikan – so named because its form resembles that of the native bird with outstretched wings – is the work of the Danish designer Finn Juhl (1912–89) and is a forerunner of the organic, sculptural forms that came to dominate furniture design during the mid-20th century. Said to have been influenced by contemporary abstract art and, in particular, the work of the German sculptor Jean Arp (1886–1966), the reclining seat and curvaceous, all-embracing back of this chair appear as one single moulded form atop four sturdy wooden legs. Its appeal is instant and welcoming, and few can resist the temptation to try it out.

One of the earliest figures to gain international acclaim for Danish design – later champions include Hans Wegner, Arne Jacobsen and Verner Panton (see pages 206, 220–3 and 254) – Finn Juhl is widely recognized as a pioneer of Modernism in Denmark. An architect by profession, he received no official training in furniture design. Instead, like many Danish artists and architects before him, he simply observed a native tradition of designing his own furniture. Where he broke with tradition, however, was by overlooking established conventions of furniture design and embracing a more modern approach to produce his uniquely sculptural pieces.

While Juhl's furniture is indeed minimalist in appearance, there is also a beautifully sculptural, organic quality to his work, which moves away from the purely functional aspect of Modernism and emphasizes the form of a piece over its function. His Pelikan is no exception in this respect. Part of his success in this and subsequent furniture designs lies in a collaboration with the cabinet-maker Niels Vodder lasting more than 20 years, from 1937–59. Designing, making and selling his own pieces from his shop in Copenhagen, Vodder became renowned for the quality and workmanship of his furniture. His reputation drew designers such as Juhl, who commissioned him to make their pieces, often relying on his skill as a craftsman to bring their ideas to fruition.

Today the Pelikan is produced under licence by the Danish firm Hansen & Sorensen and is widely available in a range of soft-toned fabrics and with legs made from various woods. But this has not always been the case. First shown at the annual Copenhagen Cabinet-Makers' Guild exhibition in 1940, a pair of dark red upholstered Pelikan chairs were two of just four that were made originally (the second pair was upholstered in black leather). Today, the whereabouts of three of these now hugely desireable and significantly valuable original Pelikans is known. The fourth, however, remains tantalizingly lost!

Above
Pioneering the organic-like curves of a Mid-Century Modern design, Pelikan reassesses form over function.

Grass-seated Chair / 1944

George Nakashima (1905–90) first made a prototype for this grass-seated chair in 1944, and his studio continues to make it to this day. Like much of Nakashima's work, the chair combines unique Japanese aesthetics of purity, grace and subtlety with an enthusiasm for traditional craftsmanship, epitomizing the American Crafts Revival of the mid-20th century.

Nakashima was born in the United States to Japanese parents, which goes some way towards explaining the melding of the two aesthetics. However, he also learned his craft under the tutelage of Gentaro Hikogawa while interred under US law during World War II. Hikogawa introduced him to the tools and techniques of traditional Japanese furniture-making, many of which are evident in his designs. For example, the use of grass (originally bailing twine, woven by his wife Marion for the prototype of 1944) and the visible joinery in this chair are typically Japanese.

Underpinning Nakashima's work was a deep, self-expressed fondness and respect for wood or, more precisely, trees. Favouring rich-coloured hardwoods, notably redwood, birch and, as in this chair, walnut, he oversaw the milling process time and again, saying that it was a crucial part of the process and akin to cutting diamonds. He also felt his designs gave a tree a second life, and a good number of his pieces reflect this quite explicitly. For example, the free-form tabletops for which he is best-known are made from untrimmed, butterfly-jointed boards, their edges left rough with all manner of burls, knots and fissures visible.

Believing that work and life should be integrated equally, Nakashima preferred to work on a domestic scale from a studio in Pennsylvania, where he employed a small number of exceptionally skilled, like-minded craftsmen. In most cases originally custom-made for site-specific commissions, many Nakashima pieces – which include desks, sideboards and cabinets, as well as tables and chairs – are still produced today under the direction of his daughter Mira.

The grass-seated chair has proved one of the most popular and commercially successful of these pieces, and it is very easy to understand why. First and foremost it looks custom-made and hand-crafted, it looks exclusive, rather than mass-produced. It also employs strong geometric forms in its component parts to great effect. Combining spindle legs, stretchers, and arm and rail supports of tapered circular section with a bentwood demi-lune top rail, and juxtaposing these with an almost-slab-like rectangular seat, gives the chair an impressive clarity of design and an appealingly confident posture. There is also considerable tactile pleasure to be had from its smooth, warm-coloured, subtly figured walnut surfaces, and from a supportive seat and back that allows you to sit in comfort and alert.

Above
Although the seat of the wartime prototype chair was covered with bailing twine, subsequent versions are finished with sea grass.

LCW / 1945–6

A perfect balance of laid-back casualness and stylish form, the LCW ('Lounge Chair Wood') was Charles and Ray Eames's first real success story. Indeed, *Time* magazine called the LCW the 'best design of the 20th century', and it set the template for all the couple's masterpieces of Mid-Century Modernism. From the DAR chair to the lounge chair and ottoman (see pages 210 and 230), the Eameses returned again and again to its cradling form – a design that was way ahead of anything that was being produced in Europe in the 1940s, it put the American husband-and-wife team on the path to becoming two of the most influential designers of all time.

The couple met at the Cranbook Academy of Art, a progressive design school in Michigan. Charles (1907–78), who originally trained as an architect, had been fashioning chairs from plywood. Ray (1912–88), an abstract artist, had been making plywood sculptures. Like many designers of the time, they were keen to exploit the plastic properties of new types of plywood in design applications. When the newly married couple moved to Los Angeles in 1941, they installed in their spare bedroom a makeshift press that they had built out of scrap wood and a bicycle pump. Dubbed the 'Kazam! Machine', it enabled the Eameses to experiment with bending plywood into three-dimensional shapes, using wood and glue (from the MGM film set where Charles worked) smuggled in under cover of darkness, to avoid alerting their landlord. Their initial product line was not in fact chairs, but lightweight moulded plywood splints, for wartime use by the US Navy. After the war, however, they were able to reapply their pioneering work in moulding plywood to furniture design.

Inspiration for the form of the LCW came from the most unlikely source: the gentle curving shape of the potato crisp. The result was a chair with a separate back and seat, each with softly undulating and rounded lines, that gives the hard plywood an inviting, comfortable appearance. The seat rests on two U-shaped plywood base pieces, each forming a pair of legs, while the back is joined to the seat by an elegantly curving 'spine' known as a lumbar support. Ingeniously, the Eameses used rubber discs called shock mounts to fix the back and seat to the lumbar support and base, making the chair more flexible as well as more comfortable – and creating one of the first examples of a responsive back rest in the history of furniture.

In 1946 the Museum of Modern Art in New York held an exhibition, 'New Furniture Designed by Charles Eames', featuring prototypes of the couple's plywood pieces. The LCW caught the eye of the furniture manufacturer Herman Miller, who bought the licence to manufacture the chair and put it into production right away. The Eameses created variations on their successful design, including a dining-chair version (DCW) and versions with a metal base and lumbar support (LCM and DCM). Original plywood finishes include cherry, walnut and ash. An LCW in birch is also now available stained in bright colours such as red, yellow and green.

Charles and Ray Eames strove to provide comfortable, stackable chairs that would be easy to mass-produce and therefore affordable. In that they succeeded, and in the process they not only pioneered the technique of body-moulding plywood, but also created a form-fitting chair with an organic quality and an elegance that are as impressive as its exceptional functionality.

Above
Fashioned from moulded plywood and attached via rubber shock mounts, the LCW's 'spine' provides what was pioneering flexible lumbar support.

Womb / 1946–8

Finland-born US-based architect and designer Eero Saarinen (1910–61) designed the Womb chair after Florence Knoll, co-founder of the furniture manufacturer Knoll Associates, challenged him to produce a chair that she could curl up in. Saarinen was certainly qualified: six years earlier, in 1940, the moulded plywood chair he designed in collaboration with Charles Eames had won first prize at the Museum of Modern Art's prestigious Organic Design in Home Furnishings competition. The Womb chair requested by Florence Knoll was to receive even greater plaudits.

Underpinning the design of the Womb was Saarinen's methodical approach to the ergonomics of seating. Rather than start from a theoretical position of how humans are supposed to sit, he spent many hours observing and sketching the numerous different ways we actually sit in a chair. This research was then tailored to his aesthetic principle that 'a chair should not only look well as a piece of sculpture in a room when no one is in it, it should also be a flattering background when someone is in it'.

In terms of component parts, the result of Saarinen's approach to design was a seat of moulded, reinforced fibreglass and a matching moulded plywood ottoman, both enclosed in foam and augmented with separate seat, back and ottoman cushions of polyester fibre over a foam core. Nowadays covered in a wide range of coloured Knoll textiles, or leather, the seat and ottoman are supported on a slender framework of bent steel rods finished in polished chrome (as here) or a matt black powder coating. The Womb is now produced in three sizes: standard, medium and child's, the latter without an ottoman.

Beyond the nuts and bolts of the composition, Saarinen more than met his aesthetic brief. Womb's broad moulded seat shell, with its fluid folds and curves, presents a particularly elegant organic form, which is augmented by the limbs of the underlying steel frame. Although the limbs are almost insect-like in their slenderness, their wide solid stance enhances, both literally and visually, the supremely supportive qualities of the chair – qualities that far exceed Florence Knoll's original ergonomic brief. You can not only curl up, but also sit, slouch, lie, sprawl, relax or sleep in great physical comfort, especially when the chair is combined with the ottoman. The comfort is also psychological: the aptly named Womb chair gives the occupant, in Saarinen's own words, 'a sublime feeling of security'.

Above right
Finished in polished chrome, the underlying steel rods of the Womb chair and ottoman terminate in stainless-steel and nylon glides, articulated to accommodate uneven floor surfaces.

Peacock (PP550) / 1947

The elegant Peacock chair is the work of one of Denmark's most prolific and influential designers: Hans Wegner (1914–2007). Wegner designed the Peacock in 1947, three years before his rise to international fame following worldwide acclaim for his Round chair of 1949 (see page 212); however, the Peacock was not his first chair. He had been designing them from his own practice as early as 1943 and, before that, as an employee at Arne Jacobsen's architectural practice in Aarhus.

Along with Arne Jacobsen and also Finn Juhl (see pages 193 and 220–3), Hans Wegner is one of several designers credited with having developed the Danish Modern style of the middle of the century. While fully embracing the tenets of functionalism so perfectly encapsulated in the work of pioneers of Modernism such as Mies van der Rohe and Le Corbusier (see pages 158, 162 and 166), Wegner was reluctant to turn his back on centuries of tradition in Danish furniture-making – he was himself trained as a cabinet-maker. More than any other designer of his generation, he combined exceptional craftsmanship with his own take on Modernism to produce pieces that were at once elegant and beautiful, and yet truly minimalist, fulfilling his desire to reduce the chair to the simplest possible form.

A perfect example of this, the Peacock is Wegner's re-interpretation of the English Windsor chair (see page 64) – traditionally a rustic form, in which the socketing of the legs and spindles directly into the seat of the chair is a common feature. Wegner's example gives the form an instant contemporary lift with a wide, low seat and beautifully exaggerated hooped back. The frame and seat are made of naturally pale turned and steam-bent ash, with darker coloured teak armrests adding a hint of contrast. While traditional Windsor chairs often have saddle-shaped seats, the Peacock's seat is woven with paper cord.

Each of the spindles has a flattened section that makes the back of the chair more comfortable and more visually interesting. Spanning the width of the chair in an arc that mirrors the shape of the hooped rail, this feature gives the chair the appearance of a peacock's tail, fanned in graceful display. Interestingly the name of the chair did not come from Wegner himself – he gave his designs serial numbers (in this case PP550) – but from his friend and fellow designer Finn Juhl, who commented on the chair's likeness to the eponymous bird.

That peacock back is objectively impressive and undoubtedly the most prominent feature. It is therefore a little ironic that the Peacock was one of several attempts by Wegner to design chairs that had 'no backs'. Of course, by that he meant that, no matter where a viewer was standing, the chair would always be pleasing to look at. Wegner succeeded: regardless of the angle, the Peacock just never disappoints.

Above
A re-interpretation of the traditional Windsor chair, the Peacock's legs, spindles, arm supports and stiles are all socketed into the seat.

Three-legged Chair / 1947

One of the most visually arresting designs of the mid-20th century, Joaquim Tenreiro's masterly three-legged chair became a design icon as soon as it appeared, in 1947. Simultaneously it references the past while pushing towards the future, a hallmark of Tenreiro's work. In this case, the past is evoked through the scale and height of the chair, which are those of a decorative slipper chair, popular during the early 19th century. Yet its angular shape and the sense of movement imparted by its linear decoration herald the future of design – the jet-propelled, space-age momentum that was to come in the 1950s and 1960s.

Just as significantly, the chair has been made with logic-defying craftsmanship. Born in Portugal into a family of woodworkers, Tenreiro (1906–92) had a profound understanding of wood. After emigrating to Brazil as a young man, he adapted his techniques to the country's indigenous hardwoods. Technically, the different hardwoods used in the three-legged chair should expand and contract at different rates, causing fissures. Yet Tenreiro's innate feel for the material and his prowess as a craftsman allowed him to overcome what for many would have been a major obstacle.

Like most designers from Brazil, Tenreiro was consistently inspired by the country's natural resources. This particular example of the three-legged chair showcases five Brazilian hardwoods – imbuia, roxinho, jacaranda, ivory (pau marfim) and cabreuva – in a stunning array of colours and grains bonded together, and hand-carved into a cohesive form. Along the side of the chair, the wider cross-sections further highlight the rich combination of materials.

Despite its immediate visual impact, this chair, like all pieces designed and made by Tenreiro, only fully reveals itself through repeated viewing and handling. When it was exhibited at the Modern Art Salon in Rio de Janeiro in 1961 the *Jornal de Brasil* described it as 'Tenreiro's spectacular chair, perfectly crafted, beautifully shaped, on which one would prefer not to sit, in order to stand back and admire it for its own sake'. Partly true, but not totally: people are also invariably drawn to sit in it, and to touch it. Indeed, it has an almost irresistible tactility, which emanates from its sensuously smooth surfaces and its carefully carved soft curves.

Tenreiro created pieces of furniture ideally adapted to urban living and a tropical climate. He also wanted his furniture to exude a feeling of 'lightness, which has nothing to do with weight but with graciousness and a functionality of space'. That he succeeded so emphatically makes the fact that Tenreiro never sold these three-legged chairs – they were designed as gifts for clients who'd commissioned a number of pieces from his atelier – immensely frustrating for a would-be owner of what have become very rare but highly coveted examples of Brazilian Mid-century Modernism.

Above right
The contrasting colours and varied figuring of the five different hardwoods employed in Tenreiro's design become even more prominent when the chair is viewed in profile.

DAR / 1948

Conceived two years prior to its launch in 1950, the DAR by Charles and Ray Eames (1907–78 and 1912–88) consistently features on lists of the most innovative furniture designs of the 20th century. Standing for 'Dining Armchair Rod' – 'Rod' refers to the metal struts that comprise the leg base supporting the seat – the DAR bears all the hallmarks of Mid-Century Modernism. In particular, the shape of the seat, which is moulded to conform to the contours of the body, is one of the pioneering examples of the organic-like forms that were to become such a feature of 1950s design. It was also the first one-piece plastic chair to be left uncovered by upholstery, but what really makes the DAR revolutionary is that it was the first predominantly plastic chair ever to be mass-produced. Cheap, portable and easy to clean, it has subsequently sold in the millions and has had an enduring effect on both domestic and office seating.

DAR's innovative design grew out of Charles and Ray Eames's pioneering experiments with moulding and bending plywood, which gained them a contract with the US Navy during World War II (see their LCW chair on page 200). After peace was declared, the US government was keen to harness wartime innovation to meet the expanding population's need for household goods, and it was in this context that the DAR was one of a range of designs that the couple entered in a competition for low-cost furniture staged by the Museum of Modern Art in New York in 1948 – the grant they won allowing them to create the prototypes for mass production.

Originally the Eameses had not considered using plastic for their range because applications of this material were still relatively new. Early trial models featured moulded steel and aluminium seats with metal and wooden bases, but in 1950 they finally switched to moulded fibreglass-reinforced plastic for the seats. The cutting-edge furniture manufacturer Herman Miller put the range into production the same year, and the rest is, as they say, history.

Wiry yet robust, the chromed metal struts that comprise the base of the DAR shown here were appositely named after the Eiffel Tower. The Plastic Shell Group, as the range was called, offered the 'Eiffel Tower' base as one of a number of metal-base options, and the shells also came in a choice of colours. Options included the DSR ('Dining Sidechair Rod'), RAR ('Rocking Armchair Rod') and LAR ('Lounge Armchair Rod').

Interestingly, the La Chaise lounge chair from the range, which had an elongated and overtly amoeba-like seat, was for a long time considered too difficult to manufacture, but was finally put into production by the European furniture company Vitra in the 1990s. Met with instant critical acclaim, its highly distinctive form was employed in an advertisement by the fashion designer Tom Ford while he was working for Gucci. Its sister DAR, some 60 years after conception, remains equally applauded and even more commercially successful. No doubt helped by the introduction of a softer polypropylene seat for improved comfort, it remains an enduringly desirable icon of Mid-Century Modern design.

Above
DAR's interlaced chromed or brushed steel 'Eiffel Tower' base provides a stable and deceptively strong base for the moulded polypropylene seat.

The Round Chair / 1949

Hans Wegner (1914–2007) was one of just a handful of furniture designers from the mid-20th century who were cabinet-makers by training. He was also a champion of the hugely influential Danish Modern style, which took the world by storm in the 1950s and 1960s. The Round Chair (PP501), conceived in 1949, was not his first chair design – earlier examples included the Peacock in 1947 (see page 206) – but it has certainly become his most famous. When it was featured on the front cover of American *Interiors* in 1950, the magazine heralded it as the 'most beautiful chair in the world'. The Round Chair instantly became an icon of its era, famously propping the historic televised presidential debate between Richard Nixon and John F Kennedy in 1960. In fact, the chair was so recognizable at that time it became known simply as 'The Chair'.

Like a number of chairs Wegner designed in the 1940s – including the best-selling Wishbone, or Y-chair, also of 1949 – the basic form of The Round Chair was inspired by paintings of Danish merchants sitting on Chinese Ming Dynasty chairs. Raised on four turned and tapering legs, which also serve as stiles and arm supports, its low, curved back rail extends to form the arms of the chair in one beautifully sculpted piece, while the gently undulated seat is covered with hand-woven cane. (Wegner also produced a model in 1950, the PP503, that had an upholstered pad seat.) Significantly, the chair encloses, but does not tightly embrace, the sitter, thereby allowing considerable freedom of movement: the comfort of a chair was as important to Wegner as its functionality (see also his Ox chair, page 258). Overall, the chair displays an almost exquisite purity in its form and its use of natural materials, but also a tactile, organic aesthetic that encapsulates the best Danish design of this period.

When asked about his chairs, Wegner is reported to have said that he wanted 'to cut down to the simplest possible elements of four legs, a seat and combined top rail and armrest'. Fuelled by a desire to design the perfect chair, and with more than 500 designs from a career spanning more than half a century, it was obviously not a challenge he took lightly. With the design of The Round Chair in particular, one can conclude that it was a challenge he met most handsomely.

Right
Now made in oak, ash, mahogany or cherry, The Round Chair's subtle decoration resides in the natural figuring of the wood.

Diamond / 1950–2

It is no surprise that one of the bestsellers in the Diamond range, designed by Harry Bertoia (1915–78) and produced by Knoll, is the children's chair. Anyone, young or old, can appreciate the magic of a range of chairs that, as Bertoia once said, 'are made mainly of air'.

The Italian-born Bertoia moved to the United States in 1930 where, nine years later, he enrolled at the progressive Cranbrook Academy of Art in Michigan. Here he met Charles Eames and Eames's future wife, Ray Kaiser. Now recognized as the most important furniture designers of their era, the pair was then just starting out on their fledgling career. Bertoia enthusiastically joined in with the couple's experiments in materials and forms, and, being primarily a sculptor, proved influential in creating a new and daring language of design. When Charles and Ray Eames (who had, by then, become married) moved from Michigan to California, they persuaded Bertoia to come with them, but once there they soon went their separate ways.

An artist at heart, Bertoia was not happy with the increasingly commercial focus of the Eameses' work. Because Hans Knoll, the director of the eponymous furniture manufacturer, did not want to see Bertoia's talent as a designer lost to the world of art, he provided Bertoia with a studio and an open-ended commission to produce whatever sort of furniture he pleased.

The result was the audacious Diamond chair, a piece that satisfactorily combined a sculptor's passion for light, space and form with the more practical requirements of an item of seating. The deceptively simple shape of the chair was the result of many months of bending, welding and hammering steel mesh until a balance was found between beauty, strength and comfort. Indeed many people assume that such a beautiful object cannot be comfortable, but the Diamond provides a surprisingly snug seat.

As a chair that is virtually transparent without its cover, the Diamond has minimal visual impact on its surroundings. This, and the fact that it is equally appealing from all angles, has made it a popular chair in contemporary homes that aim for an uncluttered look. The design and materials of the chair (which proved to be Bertoia's final furniture design before he turned his attention to art full-time) also mean that it works just as well indoors as out. It is possible, as illustrated here, to get upholstered versions of the Diamond chair. This, undoubtedly, increases the comfort factor. In red leather it also adds an overt sexuality — although, ironically, for some purists only an undressed one will do.

Ant (3100) / 1952

Denmark-born Arne Jacobsen (1902-71) was already a successful architect when he came up with the design for an easy-to-produce lightweight stacking chair for the factory canteen of the Danish pharmaceutical firm Novo Nordisk. Despite its initial unpopularity, the three-legged Ant proved to be the chair that established Jacobsen as a force to be reckoned with in furniture design.

In his youth, prior to studying as an architect, Jacobsen had been an apprentice bricklayer. This hands-on training had given him a feeling for materials and generated the belief that mass-produced furniture should, if it was to be any good, have a handcrafted quality. Jacobsen pursued this ideal in the Ant with the use of moulded plywood. Although not a pioneer of moulded plywood technology – accolades that belong to the Finlander, Alvar Aalto, and the Americans Charles and Ray Eames – he quickly mastered the art of press-moulding with steam. The result was a one-piece seat and back comprising nine layers of laminated moulded veneer with two additional internal layers of cotton textile.

Slightly flexible under load, supportive and comfortable, the plywood seat and back was originally raised on tubular plastic legs, but these were soon replaced with tubular steel in a chrome or satin chrome finish, attached with simple bolts, and terminating in floor-protecting rubber caps. The overall result was a comfortable chair comprising few materials, simple to construct and therefore ideal for mass production. However, the Ant also had something else going for it: the pleasing hourglass symmetry of its zoomorphic shape. Like many of Jacobsen's other designs, the Ant (Myren in Danish) was named simply after what it looked like: white, as here, diverse colours and natural wood finishes are now available, but when seen in black lacquer the resemblance to its namesake is most evident.

Jacobsen used the Ant as a basis for many other designs, the most notable being the Series 7 range (see page 222), which he developed from 1955. The fact that the Series 7 was welcomed by one journalist as 'finally a chair by Jacobsen with four legs and with optional arms' gives an insight into why the Ant, with its three legs and lack of arms, was not widely popular straightaway. Although the use of just three legs was designed ergonomically to minimize tangling the user's feet, aesthetically it was just a bit too out-of-left-field for many. However, precedent says people usually come around … in this case to the extent that the Ant went on to become one of the most popular chairs of the 1950s and has enjoyed a notable renaissance since the new millennium. Moreover, for those still unable to come to terms with just three legs, a four-legged version (the 3101) has been available since 1980.

Above
Ant's one-piece moulded plywood seat and back is nowadays available in a wide range of lacquered colours, or natural maple or beech wood.

Series 7: No. 3107 / 1955

There is some debate surrounding the origin of what can be considered one of the most successful furniture designs of all time. While some say that Arne Jacobsen (1902–71) designed his 3107 chair as a stacking chair for Rødovre town hall (a building also designed by Jacobsen), others argue that it was commissioned from Jacobsen by the furniture manufacturer Fritz Hansen as a chair to accompany its pre-existing range of dining tables. Such uncertainty around the original intended use of the chair is testament to its versatility – one can imagine it filling either function (and many others as well) with equal ease.

The 3107 is surely one of the most user-friendly chairs ever made (explaining why it is also one of the most commercially successful chairs). The simple, curvaceous shape allows it to fit unobtrusively into most surroundings, and the gently concave moulded plywood seat makes it as comfortable as any chair you will sit in. Relatively light and solidly constructed, it is available in a vast array of colours and finishes. In short, it is an almost flawless design.

The 3107's huge success has, of course, led to numerous imitations (although a trained eye can tell the difference in an instant – their shape is usually a little lumpen compared with the original, or the plywood is crudely moulded). However, the huge number of fake 3107 chairs in existence has done little to dilute the popularity of this enduring design. One 'lookalike' that has, in fact, boosted the profile of the 3107 is the chair a naked Christine Keeler sat astride in the famous photograph by Lewis Morley. The photo of the former model, whose affair with a government minister shook the world of British politics in 1963, came to be one of the defining images of the Sixties, and the chair that starred in it shot to similar fame. Few knew that it was a cheap knockoff of the real thing, but that mattered little.

The 3107 was the chair that turned Jacobsen from a designer well known mainly in Denmark to one with a significant international status. Its appearance coincided with Scandinavian design as a whole beginning a period of unprecedented popularity. Previously a rather sheltered environment for design, Denmark and the other Scandinavian nations took the technical innovations of American designers such as Charles and Ray Eames (such as the composite moulding of plywood used for the 3107) and the forms of cutting-edge abstract artists to create an updated design style that the rest of the world welcomed with open arms.

Above
The lightly versatile 3107 is stackable up to 12 high – unlike its Series 7 sister, which has arms.

Moro / c.1955

An Italian, Piero Fornasetti (1913–88) is credited with having produced more than 11,000 designs during his lifetime, earning himself the accolade of being the most prolific designer of the 20th century. His idiosyncratic style appeared in all home wares, from umbrellas to ceramics to furniture, and did much to change the look of 1950s design. With a background in art, sculpture and engraving, Fornasetti's interest lay as much in the visual appeal of a design as in its structural integrity, and the Moro chair is a particularly fine example of this.

The great appeal here is the juxtaposition of the chair's simplicity with the surreal nature of its surface decoration. The piece has but a basic moulded plywood form, painted and lacquered, and stands on elegant, tapering legs. Nothing too remarkable there, one might say, and yet the theatricality of the 'moor' chair back, the depth of colour, the striking quality of the image – these all make for an irresistibly eye-catching piece. (You might expect to turn the chair around, to see the back of this same figure, but instead there he is again, only facing the opposite direction.)

The design is typical of much of Fornasetti's work, in particular the application of his surreal take on the artistic tradition of trompe l'oeil – the idea of giving a three-dimensional quality to something that has a two-dimensional plane. In fact, this was a technique Fornasetti exemplified in pieces of furniture he produced in collaboration with his contemporary Gio Ponti (see page 234). Of particular note among such pieces were a number of cabinets designed by Ponti, onto which Fornasetti screen-printed elaborate three-dimensional architectural images.

The Moro chair is one of several designs along a similar theme – 'theme and variation' were central tenets of Fornasetti's work – where the same basic chair form was used with differently designed chair backs. Among these were Corinthian and Ionic column designs, mythological figures representing each of the four seasons, and one bearing his popular sun motif on both seat and chair back. What is especially remarkable about the Moro chair is Fornasetti's use of colour, for much of his design work was executed simply in black and white.

Originally, Fornasetti produced his chairs in limited runs, each one marked and numbered on the back. In keeping with this tradition, Fornasetti's son Barnaba still runs the atelier in Milan and continues to reproduce his father's designs. There are so many that models are 'rested' every so often to enable others to have a turn – a clever way of maintaining the brand exclusivity and collectability of these unique designs.

Above
Repeating the Moor on both sides of the chair retains its visual presence even when the chair is pushed under a table.

Tulip Armchair / 1956

Eero Saarinen (1910–61) designed the Tulip approximately ten years after his highly praised Womb chair (see page 202) and some five years before his best-known architectural commission, the TWA Flight Centre (Terminal 5) at New York's JFK airport, which was completed in 1962, the year after his death. Core characteristics of Saarinen's work – assuaging the sometimes overly austere functionality of Modernism with the use of organic forms, and exploring the sculptural qualities of new man-made materials – are evident in all of these designs, but are particularly prevalent in the Tulip.

Produced either with armrests (as here) or without them, the Tulip was conceived as part of a range of complementary tables and chairs known as the Pedestal Group, manufactured by Knoll. The rationale of supporting both the chair seats and table tops on slim pedestal bases was informed by Saarinen's desire to remove what he believed was the confusing and restless atmosphere created in a room by the clutter of traditional chair and table legs. His intention was to 'clear out the slum of legs …[and] make the air all one thing again'. This would also help to harmonize the relationship between a table and its chairs.

Given that Saarinen believed that 'every significant piece of furniture from the past has a holistic structure', the pedestal base and the chair seat (or table top) would ideally have been one moulded plastic form. However, the technical limitations of plastics technology did not allow this. Thus, the seat shell is moulded fibreglass with a reinforced plastic-bonded finish, while the separate pedestal base is cast in aluminium with a plastic finish. The two-part construction allows for a fixed or a swivel seat, and matching the colours of the plastic finishes – either white, black or platinum – convincingly creates the illusion of a one-piece construction. The resulting smoothness and fluidity of line are accentuated by complementary or contrasting splashes of colour in the upholstery, in the form of either a C-shaped fabric- or leather-covered seat cushion or a fully upholstered inner shell.

When it first appeared, the Tulip anticipated the Space Age and, more than 50 years on, it has somehow succeeded in retaining its futuristic look, which is undoubtedly one of the factors in its enduring appeal. Yet this is a chair that seems to sit happily not only in Modern and Post-Modern interiors, but also in many older period rooms. Its timeless sculptural quality and its clarity of form do much to explain that. They also guaranteed the Tulip's elevation to the status of classic design.

Left
Part of a stylized organic composition, Tulip's streamlined folds and curves are moulded in fibreglass reinforced with a smooth monochrome plastic-bonded finish.

Lounge Chair (670) & Ottoman (671) / 1956

The Eames lounge chair with matching ottoman, Nos 670 and 671, by Charles and Ray Eames (1907–78 and 1912–88), stands out from the rest of the couple's outstanding repertoire because it is lavish, complex-looking and relatively expensive. Yet it has become one of the most cherished and instantly recognizable designs by the American husband-and-wife team. Comfortable and puffy like an old-fashioned club sofa, it is the mid-20th-century answer to the Victorian day bed.

The couple's genius lies in the fact that the chair and ottoman look equally appropriate in the executive office, a home study or the family den. There are many who grew up in the 1960s and 1970s who fondly remember putting their feet up and rocking back against the headrest, or spinning around on the swivel base like a top. But for all its relaxed styling, this ultra-modern suite made quite a worldly statement. Owning the Eames lounge chair and ottoman became a sign that you were an individual with very discerning taste.

Charles and Ray Eames had been experimenting with chair designs incorporating separate curved plywood shells for the seat, back and headrest since the 1940s. In fact, the shock mounts that allow the back rest and headrest to flex slightly in use were originally developed in 1945–6 for their LCW chair (see page 200). Charles said he wanted this chair to have the 'warm receptive look of a well-used first baseman's mitt', so they opted for moulded plywood veneered with rich, warm rosewood and combined with supple leather upholstery. For the base, tubular steel and plywood were tested and rejected, in favour of black enamel and polished aluminium. The chair's five-prong base swivels, while the four-prong base of the ottoman does not. The final prototype was produced in 1956 as a birthday gift for their friend Billy Wilder, the Hollywood film director. The furniture manufacturer Herman Miller put it into production in 1957, the same year that it won first prize at the prestigious design exhibition the Milan Triennial, and it has been in continuous production ever since.

There are more individual parts in the lounge chair and ottoman than in any other Eames design. The three curving sections of the original chair were constructed from five layers of moulded plywood, but today's versions have seven layers, and the rosewood veneer has been replaced by walnut, cherry or santos palisander (which has a similar appearance to rosewood). The classic suite came with black leather upholstery, but it is now also made in other colours, including white. Whereas the early versions had down and feathers in their padding, more contemporary examples are filled with foam.

The first lounge chair and ottoman retailed for $637, a substantial sum in 1956. It remains expensive: the main cost being for the hand labour required to assemble all the separate parts and for the upholstery work. Not that the price has ever put people off – the still prestigious lounge chair and ottoman occupy a favourite spot in thousands of home and offices around the world.

Right
Hardwood-veneered, the moulded plywood back and headrest are secured by chromed steel bars mounted on rubber shock mounts that allow slight flexing under load.

Superleggera / 1957

The Superleggera chair, by Gio Ponti (1891–1979), is that rare thing, a design that seems at once ancient and utterly contemporary. This timeless quality is a testament to Ponti's sensitivity as a designer. He managed to achieve incredible success during his lifetime not only as a furniture designer, but also as an architect, poet, writer, magazine editor, ceramicist, stage designer, town planner, painter and graphic artist. Despite this formidable talent, his designs always have a modest, approachable quality.

Ponti, as he once said, was always keen to embrace the 'most modern mechanical equipment', but he wanted to ensure that 'people retain their predominance over machinery' by adding an element of the 'human system' to his designs. The Superleggera chair is a perfect example of this approach. While the overall form of the chair is openly derived from the Chiavari chair, made by local craftsmen in the Italian coastal town of Chiavari, the refined, slender forms of his version of the vernacular style could be achieved only with the use of precision machines.

The Superleggera, which translates as 'super-light', is an adaptation of the Leggera, which Ponti had designed two years earlier. Cesare Cassina, the founder of the furniture manufacturer of the same name, had asked his close friend Ponti to design a chair that would fit comfortably into the new style of urban apartment that was springing up all over Europe. These apartments were smaller than their predecessors, and space was at a premium – hence Ponti's decision to produce a chair that was pared down to its essential elements. Amazingly, this economical approach did not lead to a compromise in style.

Of course, the key feature of the Superleggera is its weight – or rather lack of it. It weighs a mere 1.7kg (3lb 12oz), a fact that was trumpeted in the many contemporary photographs that show children lifting the chairs with their little fingers and 1950s housewives staring with astonishment at weighing hooks with the Superleggera dangling on the end.

The materials – ash, with a finely woven cane seat – were carefully chosen for their lightweight qualities. What allows such a lightweight chair to have such strength is largely the way that the thin wooden struts and rods slot together. One would, of course, need to take the chair apart to appreciate the beauty of its construction, but the fact that such a slimline chair is so stable (as attested by the fact that Ponti threw one from his fourth-floor window and it merely bounced and rolled away) tells you that there must be an ingenious designer at work – a description that certainly fits Gio Ponti.

Above
The ash wood frame, here in black lacquer, but also made in white or clear lacquer, supports a woven cane seat.

Cherner Armchair / 1957–8

Belatedly named after its American designer, the Cherner armchair had a more controversial start in life than most chairs. It was designed in the late 1950s by Norman Cherner (1920–87) for the Plycraft furniture manufacturing company. Unfortunately, Plycraft told Cherner that the project had been scrapped, then proceeded to produce the chair as its own design. This came to Cherner's attention in 1961, when the chair appeared in Norman Rockwell's painting *The Artist at Work*, printed on a cover of the widely read *Saturday Evening Post*. The chair's popularity soared, and Cherner sued. Although a settlement was reached, in the form of royalty payments, by the early 1970s Plycraft had stopped production, and for more than 20 years the Cherner was rarely found outside of design museums and the homes of a few aficionados.

In 1999, however, Norman Cherner's sons recovered their late father's designs, founded the Cherner Chair Company and renewed production. Given its design pedigree, the Cherner's rejuvenated desirability comes as no surprise. Having studied and lectured on the Bauhaus movement at Columbia University and worked as an instructor at New York's Museum of Modern Art in the late 1940s, Cherner had gone on to become a designer of furniture, glass, lighting, even toys, and also of pioneering low-cost prefabricated housing. Experience gained in these different mediums is clearly evident in the Cherner chair's appealing Mid-Century Modern form and innovative construction.

Also available as an armless side chair, and with optional leather- or fabric-upholstered seat pads and back pads, the Cherner is raised on four slender, subtly curved legs of two-piece laminated beech, veneered in beech or walnut. The one-piece seat and back is moulded from beech-laminated plywood and veneered in beech or the original walnut, or nowadays with alternative ebony, orange or white finishes. Ingeniously, the chair is of graduating thickness – from 15-ply at the slender waist, tapering to 5-ply around the perimeter of the seat. This not only gives the chair considerable structural strength, but also enhances its dramatic sculptural quality – the pinched waist and flared seat and back being noticeably anthropomorphic and decidedly female.

The sculptural qualities of the chair are further accentuated by the bentwood arms, which are fashioned from one length of solid beech and are bolted to the back and to the tops of the front legs. Their extravagant sweeping curves have a stylized organic quality often employed in Mid-Century Modern designs – and one that also recalls the flamboyant whiplash curves, suggestive of plant forms or long, flowing female tresses, found on Art Nouveau chairs some half a century earlier.

Egg / 1957–8

The Egg chair is Arne Jacobsen's inimitable take on the wing-back chair of many a traditional home. Large and voluptuous, its sculptural form embraces the sitter, cocooning him or her in the plushest comfort.

This iconic chair, originally produced in striking red upholstery, was designed by Jacobsen (1902–71) for the SAS Royal Hotel in Copenhagen, along with the Swan chair (see page 244). It is just one of the Danish architect and designer's now-legendary pieces of furniture design (see also the Ant and the Series 7 chairs, pages 220 and 222). A pioneer of the concept of 'total design', Jacobsen, who was arguably Denmark's leading exponent of the Danish Modern style, designed every last detail of the hotel – not 'just' the building itself, but everything inside it, too, from furniture and lighting to textiles and cutlery. With 21 floors, it was the tallest building in Copenhagen at the time, effectively the city's first skyscraper.

Like much of Jacobsen's work, and indeed many designs from the 1950s, the Egg chair embraced new technologies that allowed for creating seats in a single-mould form. Thought to have been inspired by Eero Saarinen's Womb chair (see page 202), it has a simple fibreglass shell covered in flexible foam that has been moulded to the shape of the human body and upholstered. It stands on an elegant steel base and, for a chair of this size – 107cm (42in) tall and weighing in at 15 kg (33lb) – it appears remarkably elegant and light.

Intended for the hotel's reception area, the chair had a sophisticated swivel function – a novelty at the time – and could be tilted back for even greater lounging comfort. The swivel aspect of the chair allowed users to turn towards each other for lively conversation, but also to turn away for a moment of privacy out of the hubbub of endless comings and goings so familiar to hotel life.

Originally produced by Fritz Hansen, the Danish furniture company with whom Jacobsen had a long-standing collaboration, the chair is still produced by the firm under licence. Sadly, this is not the case for the original Egg sofa, several of which also graced the lobby area of the hotel. Producing these proved too costly, and they have not been made since the 1950s – existing examples remain rare. Instantly recognizable today, however, the Egg chair has become a popular icon, familiar to many in advertisements and films, and lately in some McDonald's restaurants!

Swan / 1957–8

The Danish architect and designer Arne Jacobsen (1902–71) had a gift for producing iconic, sculptural forms that remain timeless classics to this day, and the Swan chair, bearing the understated elegance that is present in so much of his work from this era – architectural or otherwise – is certainly no exception. Seen in profile, the chair resembles the form of the graceful bird from which it takes its name. Sitting neatly on a cast-aluminium star-footed base, the seat sweeps up at the sides to form two wing-like armrests, while the chair back rises from a narrow waist and widens at the top to embrace the sitter.

Jacobsen's designs epitomized the modern Scandinavian trend that surfaced at the beginning of the 1940s in the work of the Danish designer Finn Juhl (see page 194) and continued well into the 1950s. Like Juhl's furniture, Jacobsen's work embodies a characteristically Danish interpretation of Modernist design. While adhering to the concepts of simple structure and new technologies, his pieces also have a sculptural, organic aesthetic that is absent in the work of more functionalist designers such as Le Corbusier and Mies van der Rohe (see pages 158, 162, 166 and 176).

Jacobsen's early chairs – the Ant from 1952 (see page 220) and the Series 7 from 1955 (see page 222) – were exemplary in their simple form, in which the chair seat and back were made from a single moulded and laminated sheet of plywood. The Egg (see page 241) and the Swan followed swiftly, and in these Jacobsen set his mind to a new challenge, namely that of producing forms consisting of only curved lines. Where the Ant and Series 7 had been two-dimensional in profile, the Swan and Egg were now three-dimensional.

The Swan, like the Egg, was an integral feature of the Danish architect's design for the SAS Royal Hotel in Copenhagen (1956–60), at which room 606 remains intact to this day. A low-slung lounge chair, the Swan complemented the more formal, upright design of the Egg, and was designed for use in public lounge areas and private suites. It also made its way up to the top floor of the 21-storey hotel, where it graced the floor of a fabulous panoramic bar.

Both chairs employed the same, innovative techniques for manufacture, which lent themselves so appropriately to Jacobsen's sculptural forms. These involved producing a fibreglass frame – one single mould for both seat and chair back – with a pliable foam covering, made by heat-treating polystyrene pellets. Jacobsen's original designs used leather upholstery, although the cost implications prohibited this, and fabric was used instead. Jacobsen also designed the Swan in sofa form, which the furniture manufacturer Fritz Hansen revived in the 1980s and continues to make, along with the chair, to this day.

Above
The sculptural bird-like form underpins the overt three-dimensionality of Jacobsen's design.

Aluminium & Soft Pad Group Chairs / 1958–69

Both the low-back chair with black leather upholstery opposite, and its high-back, brown-leather sister are from a range of chairs called the Soft Pad Group that was introduced in 1969 by the American designers Charles and Ray Eames (1907–78 and 1912–88). However, the basic structure of the chairs – lightweight swivel aluminium frame, five-footed aluminium base (available with or without castors) and, crucially, an upholstery suspension system – is identical to those in the range of hugely innovative chairs known as the Aluminium Group that was developed by the Eameses eleven years earlier, in 1958. The Soft Pads are thus simply variants of the original Aluminium models, and the only difference lies in the former's use of soft pad cushions on the seat and back.

It is immediately evident that these chairs have that winning combination of classic yet contemporary looks that has made them so appealing for executive office use. It is ironic then, that their design roots could not be further from the boardroom. Charles and Ray Eames initially designed the Aluminium Group for outdoor use. When their friends Eero Saarinen and Alexander Girard designed a home, Miller House, for the industrialist Irwin Miller in Columbus, Indiana, the Eameses were commissioned to produce some weather-resistant furniture for the patio. The result was a group of chairs not only suitable for exterior use, but also interior – a versatility exploited by the manufacturers Herman Miller, who initially marketed them as the Indoor-Outdoor Group.

Underpinning the enduring commercial success of the chairs was the Eameses design ethos, in which they prized practicality above beauty. As Ray Eames once said: 'What works is better than what looks good,' adding, 'the "looks good" can change, but what works, works.' In this case, the first thing that worked was the aluminium frame. Comprising one-piece curved aluminium side ribs and arms on an aluminium base, it makes for a strong, lightweight chair that is easy to move – especially when using it's back stretcher as a carrying handle. Even more impressive is the unique suspension system in which a continuous length of seat-back fabric is stretched taut between the aluminium side ribs and subtly conforms to the shape of the sitter. In addition to its functionality – it provides very comfortable support – this represented a major departure from the Eameses previous chair designs (see the LCW on page 200, the DAR on page 210, and the Lounge Chair on page 230) in which the seat and back were conceived as a solid shell.

As Ray Eames said 'the "looks good" can change', and thus there are various options as far as the upholstery is concerned. Whether in a woven fabric or leather, the best-known look – a very clean, linear one – is for these to be horizontally ribbed at just under 5cm (2in) intervals from the front of the seat to the top of the back. The alternative is a synthetic Cygnus mesh fabric, which is self-contouring, provides aeration, is slightly translucent and gives the chair a lighter feel. The third option, the Soft Pad shown here, is plusher, more cosseting and, indeed, more executive or boardroom than open-plan. To celebrate the Aluminium Group's 50th birthday, Herman Miller even produced a special edition leather pads in an iridescent pearl finish. Certainly a fantastic collector's item, but as a range rejuvenating device it simply wasn't required: the Aluminium and Soft Pad Group chairs not only helped define the Mid-Century American Modern look, but they continue to hold sway over the office aesthetics of today.

Above
Bolted to the arms, side ribs are all one-piece cast in lightweight but strong aluminium, and provide anchorage for the unique upholstery suspension system.

Cone / 1958

Is the Cone actually a chair? Its designer, Danish-born Verner Panton (1926–98), blatantly challenged all conventional notions of how a chair should look. Many critics argue that his 'chairs' are not chairs at all; chairs, by definition, should have legs, therefore Panton's creations are seats. Such analysis seems petty, but nevertheless it was this kind of issue that fuelled and provoked Panton into uncharted areas of experimentation and technical abandon. More specifically, his work with the Danish architect Arne Jacobsen and his close relationship with designers such as Poul Henningsen strongly influenced his industrial aesthetic and use of sometimes uncompromising and unconventional materials.

The Cone chair quickly defined Panton. The furniture manufacturer Fritz Hansen had put Panton's first two pieces of furniture, the Bachelor and Tivoli chairs, into production in 1955, but, although they were a commercial success, neither could compete with the sheer originality of the Cone. Panton designed it for his parents' new restaurant. Constructed of thin sheet steel with a padded exterior, it was comfortable, striking and futuristic. The chair is so fluid that it appears to be seamless. Viewed from almost any angle, it has a sense of being formed as one piece, while the low profile of the quadruped base gives it a gravity-defying appearance. Panton was intent on injecting colour and form into both the commercial and domestic interior, and the Cone fulfilled both criteria, suiting the dining table or the desk.

In 1961, when it was photographed for the Danish design magazine *Mobilia*, Panton caused a minor outrage by draping the chairs with naked models and shop mannequins. On another occasion a whole street in New York came to a standstill when crowds gathered to look at the chair in a shop window. He was ever intent on pushing the boundaries, and such publicity only helped to ensure his place in design history. The success gave him greater scope for experimentation, and variations on the Cone theme soon followed in 1959 with the Heart Cone and the Wire Cone.

Panton's popularity faded somewhat throughout the 1980s, but in the following decade the resurgence in popularity of Mid-Century Modernism saw his designs once again take centre stage. A British *Vogue* cover in 1995 heralded a comeback for the master of Pop Futurist design, and his catalogue is now produced by the design company Vitra. The Cone comes in no fewer than nine colours, although modern manufacturing processes mean that the body is now of laminated construction. The matching footstool makes an excellent complement and also works well as a stand-alone piece.

Right
Based on a classic geometric figure – a cone – the chair's laminate body is softened with a circular seat squab and polyurethane foam upholstery.

Panton / 1960

In a world where achievement is measured by 'firsts', the Panton chair crossed a boundary in design that had previously thwarted many other talented architects and designers of the 20th century. Producing a single-piece injection-moulded plastic chair, using largely unproven modern materials, was a concept that had obsessed the Danish designer Verner Panton (1926–98). The protracted development phase of this chair can be charted from the evolution of the early prototypes in 1959–60 until August 1967, when the official launch of the classic Panton chair in the Danish design journal *Mobilia* gave the world one of the most iconic chairs in history.

An innovative and forward-thinking designer, Verner Panton was consistently brilliant in both architecture and design, encompassing all disciplines from lighting and furniture to complete environments. Although the Panton chair is similar in design and concept to his single-form plywood S chair (initially developed in 1956 and a first in chair design), a pile of plastic buckets was reportedly the inspiration for the sleek, sexy Panton chair. It stacks effortlessly, and the varied palette of colours that it comes in, including a rich red and a bright yellow, has cemented its sinuous cantilevered profile in the minds of Pop-aesthetic lovers. Indeed, it epitomizes the ideals of the 1960s Pop aesthetic, and like all good design combines functionality with form. Ironically, although Pop was a disposable culture manufactured from materials with a supposedly short life span, the thinking behind these ideals has become the *raison d'être* for their longevity.

Original 1960s Pantons are rare nowadays, but the chair's iconic status has ensured ongoing production. Indeed, currently manufactured by Vitra in two plastic variants, it has been through four distinct manufacturing phases utilizing different types of plastic – commercial testament to the enduring strength of the design and the continuing demand for it.

The Panton chair was both a technical triumph and an instant success. Its form graced the pages of design journals and magazines the world over. There were the classic image of Marianne Panton sitting in the futuristic dining room designed by her husband and the infamous 1970 fashion feature in the British magazine *Nova* showcasing the chair under the headline 'How to Undress in Front of Your Husband'. In 1995, the cover of British *Vogue* showed the model Kate Moss sitting naked on a Panton chair. Panton's furniture also featured in Stanley Kubrick's visionary film *2001: A Space Odyssey*. With such an impressive visual back catalogue, it would be fair to say that words are not really needed to describe or indeed justify the Panton – all one needs to do is stand back and look.

Ox (EJ100) / 1960

Something of a departure for Hans Wegner (1914–2007), the Ox is a masterful leather-clad beast of a chair, majestic and domineering. Although the vast majority of this Danish designer's chairs are relatively small-scale and made from beautifully crafted wood (see the Peacock and The Round Chair, pages 206 and 212), this piece nevertheless bears some of the characteristic features of his work.

Of immediate interest is the chair's arresting appearance. It is crafted as a single form, with the seat, arms and back all appearing as one seamless sculptural flowing shell – a common theme during the 1950s and 1960s, and one that epitomizes Wegner's desire to reduce the chair to its simplest form. Taking its name from the unusually wide headrest, which resembles the horns of an ox, the design was inspired by Wegner's admiration of the work of Pablo Picasso. A personal favourite of Wegner's, the chair is upholstered in ox leather, in keeping with his meticulous attention to detail. Almost a cubic metre in size, it is every inch a statement piece and needs a good-sized space to sit in, yet the simple chromed tubular-steel legs prevent it from looking too solid or heavy. Indeed, the original chair was reputedly rather lightweight, being constructed predominantly of foam padding over a wooden frame.

Wegner was a master of combining the function of a piece with its aesthetic appeal, without sacrificing either. One of the challenges he set himself in his quest to design the perfect chair was to produce a form that could be used in different ways, in order to provide comfort for the sitter no matter what his or her position. Looking at the Ox chair, you can imagine curling up in the embrace of the chair's huge form, or perhaps draping yourself across it with your legs hanging over the side. For even more luxurious lounging, a matching ottoman is available.

First produced in 1960, the Ox chair proved just too avant-garde for its time. It was not popular with the consumer and, by 1962, had gone out of production. In 1985, however, Wegner revived the design, with the help of the Danish furniture manufacturer A P Stolen, and it has been in production ever since. It is currently available in a range of colours, but the original black seems a must for capturing the Ox's intended masculinity.

Karuselli / 1963

The Karuselli is a statement chair. Not one to hide coyly in a corner of the living room, this chair, by the Finnish designer Yrjö Kukkapuro (b. 1933), demands a great amount of space and catches the eye with its cavernous seat and single webbed foot. For its designer, the chair was a statement that the time for fibreglass – long seen as the material of the future – had finally arrived. 'I was always dreaming of making fibreglass chairs,' Kukkapuro once said, 'but the dream was little short of utopia in the Finland of those days.'

The dream became reality after many years of hard graft as well as reverie. When Kukkapuro developed a technique to produce a chair in fibreglass, all he then needed was inspiration for the form it should take. There are two versions of the next instalment of the Karuselli story, but both take place in the snowy environs of his homeland. One says that while playing with his daughter at making 'snow chairs' he hit upon the Karuselli shape. The other version has Kukkapuro taking a mould from an impression that he left in the snow after falling over (and falling asleep) on his way back from a particularly drunken party. Whichever of the two is true (and perhaps Kukkapuro adapted the story according to the listener), it is clear that he wanted to make a seat that embraced the human form. 'A chair should be as softly shaped as people are,' Kukkapuro once said, 'and if at all possible, just as beautiful.'

The chair is called Karuselli, which means 'carousel', because it swivels (and rocks). Its construction is complex, involving a steel-reinforced fibreglass base with a steel cradle and a steel-reinforced moulded-plastic fibreglass shell seat. This is finished with foam-backed leather upholstery, with the leather being attached with press studs for easy removal.

The success of the Karuselli was immediate. Another of Kukkapuro's stories has it that he took the prototype for the chair into the Haimi showroom for an early-morning meeting. The meeting overran, meaning that the chair was still sitting on the shop floor as the first customer came in. Needless to say, they ordered one on the spot, convincing Haimi to put the design into production. More formal praise came in 1966 when Kukkapuro won the prestigious Lunning Prize, which was awarded annually during the 1950s and 1960s to two eminent Scandinavian designers.

Still in production today (although now manufactured by Avarte), the Karuselli is Kukkapuro's most iconic piece of furniture. With its bold shape and construction, this endearing and enduring chair has the carefree optimism that defines the best 1960s designs.

Above
The profoundly comfortable Karuselli can swivel and rock on its brushed metal support.

Poltrona Moleca / 1963

Like its sister chair the Poltrona Mole ('soft armchair'), the Poltrona Moleca ('mischievous armchair') was one of a group of iconic pieces of furniture that helped to usher in an entirely new international attitude to design. Conceived by the architect Sergio Rodrigues (b. 1927) as a sumptuous yet slouchy leather cushion slung across a web of leather straps, it conforms to any body size, truly defining the lounge chair of the 1960s.

The Poltrona Moleca is also lauded for being instantly recognizable as a Brazilian design. Its peg construction borrows heavily from the indigenous furniture-making tradition in Brazil. In addition, the thick and in places bulbous rosewood that forms the chair frame is one of the materials most often used by the country's furniture makers, while the leather straps that provide the support for the seat and back are reminiscent of traditional Brazilian hammocks.

Rodrigues was fascinated by the needs of the chair's occupant – not just functional, but also aesthetic, psychological and spiritual. Like many of his designs, the Poltrona Moleca has a whimsically animated feel. There is a delightful interplay between the floppiness of the cushion and the trunk-like legs, which give the impression that they could, at any moment, walk away. The chair looks large and important, yet also sprawling and laid-back, like a banker in jeans. It speaks comfort and asks to be sat on – although it will be not so much sitting as reclining, relaxing, nesting. Indeed, in many respects the Poltrona Moleca is the Brazilian answer to a Bauhaus chair: it champions comfort over form.

Sergio Rodrigues helped to shape Brazilian homes through the latter half of the 20th century and into the 21st. Just as his architectural designs include 'kit' houses whose comfortable vernacular blends seamlessly into the terrain, so his furniture embraces and celebrates his country's culture. Thus the Poltrona Moleca speaks of the relaxed atmosphere that fosters hours of conversation, a staple of Brazilian leisure time with family and friends, while the use of native leathers and indigenous hardwoods indicates an appreciation of available natural resources and also the importance of supporting eco-conscientious industries. Equally appealing is the fact that when the Poltrona Moleca went into production each chair was handmade and overseen by Rodrigues himself – standards of craftsmanship and quality control that have ensured each example is subtly unique.

Above
Looped and buttoned into an indigenous rosewood frame, the seats leather webbing supports recall the traditional Brazilian hammock.

Ball / 1963

Perhaps more at home in a science-fiction film than the conventional living room, Eero Aarnio's Ball chair caused a sensation when it was first exhibited at the Cologne furniture fair in 1966. It has since become one of the most iconic images of what is fondly referred to as the 'space age'. And yet it might not have entered the global arena at all, had it not been for this Finnish designer's good fortune.

An extraordinary experiment in fibreglass technology, the prototype of this chair was made by Aarnio (b. 1932) for his own home in 1963. It was not until it was spotted by representatives from a furniture company interested in his other work that he was asked to produce it on a larger scale. The chair was truly innovative on so many levels that it was an immediate hit. Taken from a perfect sphere, its form was so completely original that it has not been replicated since. A slice cut from the sphere at an oblique angle created a totally internal, private space for the sitter. Not only did they sit in great comfort – all surfaces of the interior were fully upholstered – but they also sat in almost complete silence, as the enclosed form cut out sound. So personal was the space created by the ball shape that Aarnio installed a red telephone in the prototype that he made for himself. This emphasized the feeling of utter privacy, but also symbolized the melding of the very latest technology so in keeping with the futuristic buzz that accompanied this era. Supported on a metal base, the Ball chair, also known as the Globe chair, was originally made in orange, red, black or white.

Aarnio took his seminal design one step further when he designed his Bubble chair in 1968. Using the same basic form, but this time with a larger slice cut from the sphere and with acrylic as the base material, the designer created an experience for the sitter that had never been achieved before – that of being seated in a totally transparent form. Aarnio pushed this experience to the absolute limit by suspending the Bubble chair from the ceiling, giving the sitter the appearance – and feeling – almost of floating in air. It was ingenious.

Eero Aarnio was one of a handful of designers at the forefront of Scandinavian design during the 1960s, making innovative use of the new and exciting developments that were happening in fibreglass and plastics technology (see also the Karuselli by Yrjö Kukkapuro on pages 262 and the Panton by Vernor Panton on page 255). Of course Charles and Ray Eames had foreshadowed this with their experiments with fibreglass in the 1950s, but it was not until the material reached the hands of innovative Finnish designers such as Aarnio that it began to reach its full potential.

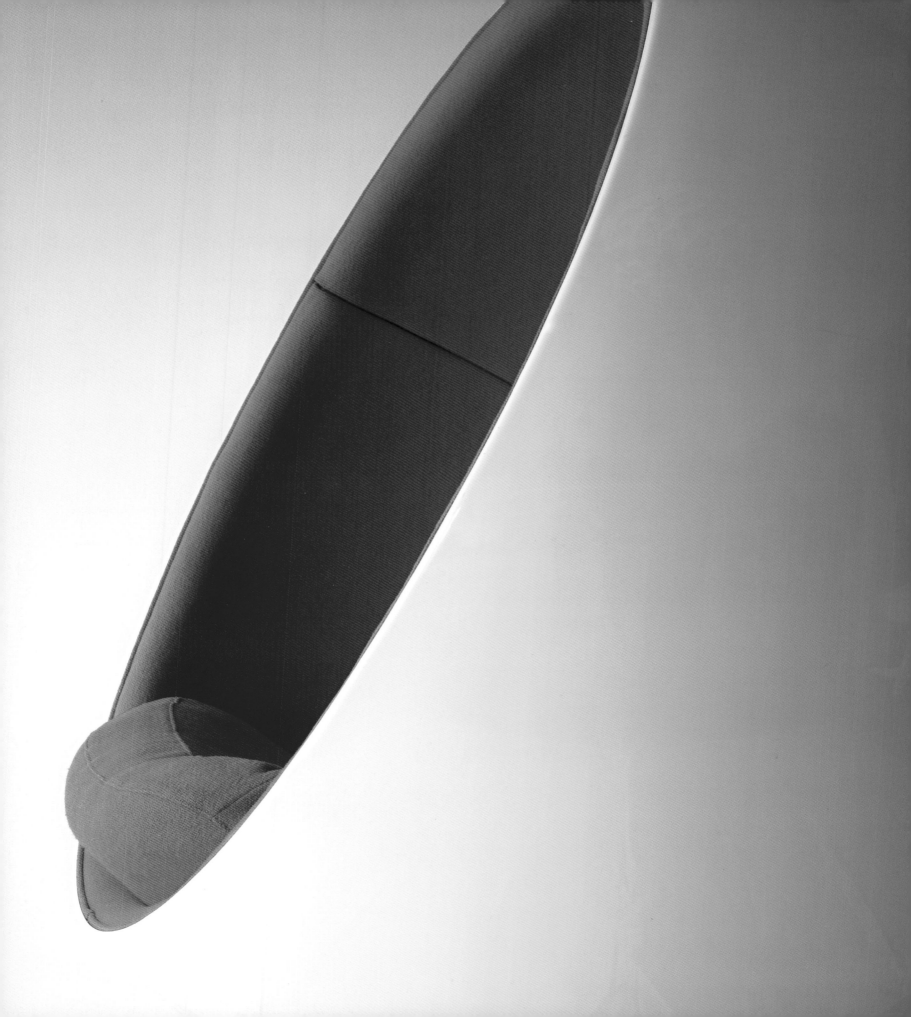

PK24 Hammock Chair / 1965

Poul Kjaerholm (1929–80) was one of the most refined Modernist designers of the 20th century, and the PK24 hammock chair is arguably his finest design. At once both modest and magnificent, its chaise longue-like form has a clarity and grace that few other furniture pieces of the period can match. Kjaerholm, who was Danish, managed to combine the typically Scandinavian skill of imbuing furniture with a warmth and earthiness with the more rigorous, purist approach pioneered by the Bauhaus in Germany.

Not only is the PK24 visually appealing, but it is also technically intelligent. It has three essential components: a long reclining cane seat, a rectangular steel base and a U-shaped steel frame which, with a little gentle tweaking of discreet runners, adjusts the seating position with a minimum of fuss. Many people have compared Kjaerholm's design with the B306 chaise longue designed in 1928 by Le Corbusier, Pierre Jeanneret and Charlotte Perriand (see page 162). However, the Dane's chaise demurely hides the mechanics of the adjustable structure, whereas the B306, with its boldly exposed steel and springs, brazenly shows it off.

It is no surprise to learn that Kjaerholm created relatively few production pieces in his lifetime. Such was his exacting nature that he preferred to pare down and refine his designs so much that he had little time in which to be prolific. He could be described as a Minimalist, but without the sterile qualities that this word often infers. His attention to detail was impeccable. A stickler for quality, he had no interest in short cuts. To buy a PK24 today (they are still produced in small numbers by Fritz Hansen, who took over the manufacture of them from E Kold Christensen in the 1970s) would cost a considerable sum. That is because the steel is not of the simple tubular variety, but a carefully calibrated flat strip style. The headrest is produced in one of the softest leathers available, and the cane seats are individually hand-woven.

The PK24's celebration of both industrial and natural materials is typical of Kjaerholm. Whereas many Scandinavian furniture designers at the time refused to look beyond the undoubted qualities of wood, Kjaerholm saw that beauty could be conjured from even the most brutal of materials.

Above
For stability, the one-piece woven cane seat and back is secured to the supporting steel frame with polished steel clips and bolts.

Plia / 1969

Designed in the late 1960s by Giancarlo Piretti (b. 1940), the Plia had a lot to live up to. Notable examples of many impressive folding chairs preceding it include the X-frame *sella curulis* magistrate's chairs of ancient Rome, the 'drunken lord' chairs of Ming Dynasty China, the campaign chairs of 19th-century European army officers and, more recently, the eponymous film director's chair. Commercial testament to the fact that the Plia has proved more than the equal of these forerunners can be found in sales of more than six million to date. Indeed, the chair's desirability was instantly evident at its launch at the Milan Furniture Fair: so many were stolen by visitors that the remainder had to be chained to the display stand.

Structurally the Plia comprises a lightweight frame of chromium-plated tubular steel, and a seat and back of translucent plastic. For comfort in use the back panel is moulded to a gentle concave curve that conforms to the horizontal curve of the human back, while the seat is moulded with a shallow circular indent to support the posterior more snugly. Centred on an ingenious three-disc hinge, the chair frame can be easily folded, when not in use, to a space-saving thickness of just 2.5cm (1in) – or 5cm (2in) at the hinge – and either propped against the wall or easily lifted and hung on a hook. Alternatively, it can be stacked unfolded.

Such comfort, versatility and efficiency of use are recurring characteristics of Piretti's chair designs – not only when he was director of research and design at Plia's Italian manufacturer, Anonima Castelli, but also later, during the late 1970s and early 1980s, when he worked with the Argentinian Emilio Ambasz on a range of office furniture that included two flexible chairs, appropriately named Vertebra and Dorsal. The appeal of the Plia, however, goes well beyond ergonomics and, indeed, its very reasonable price. Viewed from any angle, unfolded or folded, it has a visual lightness that emanates from the slenderness and light colour of the metal tubing and the translucency of the plastic. It is now available in a range of subtle tints, as well as the colourless original, but the sheer clarity and elegance of the design are what underpin the appeal of the Plia and guarantee its status as 'classic'.

Almost inevitably, alternative versions of the Plia have been produced. Some have had solid-colour polypropylene seats and backs, others wooden frames and cane seats, while recent student re-interpretations have featured carpeted upholstery, bubble-wrap covers and even basketball-net seats – cutting-edge stuff but, as with most classics, you can 'pimp the ride', but you will rarely improve on the original design.

Above
A slender chromium-plated tubular-steel frame, which folds on a compact three-disc hinge, and a translucent, subtly tinted plastic seat and back harmoniously combine to make the Plia one of the lightest chairs in production, both literally and aesthetically.

Wiggle / 1972

The Wiggle chair was designed in 1972 by the Los Angeles-based architect Frank Gehry (b. 1929) and was subsequently made by the German manufacturer Vitra. Best known for his iconic Guggenheim Museum in Bilbao, Gehry was also the architect of the Vitra Design Museum, which has a major permanent display of classic chairs from around the world.

Gehry conceived the Wiggle as part of a series of furniture (a matching Wiggle stool and a slightly smaller Wiggle side chair are also available). The range, Easy Edges, was named after the laminated material, edge board, from which it is constructed. Developed in the late 1960s by Gehry himself, and made up of layers of corrugated cardboard edged with hardboard, edge board proved very strong, relatively inexpensive and pleasantly tactile, feeling rather like corduroy. Above all, however, edge board could be manipulated into extravagant shapes, and in this respect it mirrored the innovative experiments in plastic seating of the 1960s. It also allowed Gehry to successfully resolve one of his fundamental concerns: 'to manipulate basic materials in unconventional ways to produce objects that are functional yet also visually striking'.

In terms of its basic shape, Wiggle has something in common with Verner Panton's plastic Panton chair designed in 1960 (see page 254). Made from a continuous length of material, both chairs display the fluidity of form characteristic of single-component no-joint construction. This lends them a sculptural quality that blurs the distinction between practical seating and works of art. They also have snake-like zoomorphic qualities, but, in contrast to the Panton's 'strike-a-pose' posture, the Wiggle's slinky, voluptuous curves display a greater sense of movement. Or, rather, they suggest imminent movement – Wiggle might rest coiled up in a corner but, like Kaa the python in the Disney film of Rudyard Kipling's *The Jungle Book*, you half expect all that understated power suddenly to uncoil and slither seductively towards you.

The major appeal of Wiggle – its uncannily naturalistic sculptural form – is augmented by a sweet irony. At the time Wiggle was designed, the primary ingredient of the edge board from which it is made – cardboard – had the lowly status of a cheap and disposable packaging material. As such, Gehry's seemingly incongruous use of it was knowingly tongue-in-cheek … and yet, times change. Cardboard remains relatively inexpensive, but it is now considered worth saving, or at least recycling. This extended longevity seems entirely appropriate for the Wiggle, whose status as an enduring classic is now permanently established.

Right
Wiggle's sinuous, coiled curves are constructed from Edge Board, which comprises some 60 glued layers of corrugated cardboard, running in alternate directions and edged with hardboard.

Brazilian Carved Wooden Chair / c.1975

In 1964 José Zanine Caldas (1919–2001) withdrew to the Brazilian beach town of Nova Vicosa to carve solid wood furniture. Zanine (the name by which he was known), a confirmed socialist, used common indigenous woods to make his robust 'everyman' chairs. Like many Brazilian designers, Zanine's love for his country's natural resources fuelled his imagination and guided his choices as a furniture-maker. A self-taught designer, architect and sculptor, he had a great reverence for wood and was known for a 'brutalist' style, characterised by large solid chunks of timber and the absence of joints.

As an ardent conservationist, Zanine was inspired in part by the native Brazilian tribes who had long espoused the philosophy that the objects you need can be made from what is available, particularly from materials otherwise regarded as waste. He thus pioneered a wave of furniture-making from reclaimed fallen trees and timber discarded by sawmills, employing designs that exposed and exalted the characteristics of the wood itself, including its naturally occurring curves and cracks. In so doing Zanine gave the felled trees a second life, creating from fallen palms a series of carved wooden chairs in which each is a unique sculpture.

On this example, the texture of the wood with its beautiful pitting and hatching tells a story about the tree it came from. At the same time the form of the chair mimics, in certain respects, that of the tree, gently flaring upwards from the base into the curved, hollowed-out trunk of the back. In a reversal of the 'bond with Nature and hug a tree' syndrome, the chair back also promises to hug the occupant… and, comfortingly, delivers. More surprisingly, the airiness of the palm wood imbues the chair with a lightness that is almost unique for such a solid wood construction.

Throughout the course of his career Zanine also experimented with production pieces, notably organic shapes in plywood. However, it is the more overtly sculptural raw wooden pieces such as this chair that bring out a key element of Zanine's spirit: his wonderfully sensual approach to form and function. Sadly, because his designs were made for specific projects and because he was working with a finite resource, they are all-too rare.

Indiana / 1975

A subtle reworking of a traditional Spanish café chair, the Indiana was created in 1975 by the in-house design team of the Barcelona-based furniture manufacturer Amat-3. The fact that tens of thousands of these chairs have subsequently been sold around the world for both café and residential use is essentially due to its ergonomic and aesthetic qualities. However, because of the time and the place of its conception, the Indiana has acquired a status that goes beyond commercial success.

Any chair associated with Barcelona will always have tough acts to follow. The Calvet chair of 1902 (see page 132), by the city's most revered architect, Antoni Gaudí, is an enduring symbol of the Art Nouveau style and of anthropomorphic design. Similarly, the MR90 Barcelona chair (see page 172), designed by Mies van der Rohe and Lilly Reich for the 1929 International Exhibition at Barcelona, remains an iconic emblem of Modernism. What, in comparison, does the Indiana have to offer?

Comprising a frame of anodized aluminium tubing and a seat and back rest of woven wicker, the chair has undoubted aesthetic appeal. The curvilinear one-piece construction of the back rail, arms and front legs is particularly pleasing, as is the tapering and subtly waisted wicker back rest. Together they make a major contribution to the Indiana's elegant, confident posture and, underpinned by the physical lightness of aluminium tubing, to the openness and airiness of the design. It is in these essentially esoteric qualities that the real gravitas of the chair emerges.

Designed in 1975, the year of the Spanish dictator General Franco's death, the Indiana has a lightweight, open design that somehow encapsulates the opening up of Spanish society with the re-establishment of democracy, and the concurrent re-energizing of Spanish art, industry and design at a national and international level. In addition to symbolizing that process, the Indiana would have also made a practical contribution to it. Viviana Narotzky, in her essay *The Footnote, the Chair and the City*, examines the design boom that developed in Barcelona in the late 1970s and flourished during the 1980s. She describes how 'design floated over the city as a mystical incantation exhaled by Barcelona's cultural breath … leaving its unmistakable trace as much in the furnishings as in the conversations'. In the café society of Barcelona, many of those conversations would have taken place over a drink while sitting in an Indiana.

Above right
Bolted together, the anodized aluminium tube frame of the Indiana supports a hand-woven wicker seat.

Rover / 1981

The Rover chair was the first item of furniture ever designed, and made, by Ron Arad (b. 1951). The Israeli-born Arad was a graduate of London's Architectural Association, an institution famed at the time for its emphasis on ideas over practical architecture. Arad clearly embraced this cerebral approach and produced, in 1981, a chair that had more in common with the work of Marcel Duchamp, the founding father of conceptual art, than any furniture designer that had gone before him. By utilizing what Duchamp called an *objet trouvé* – a found object (in this case a car seat) – Arad was stating that the interesting thing about his chair was not the detailing or the craftsmanship or the ergonomics, or anything else by which design is traditionally judged, but the idea.

There is a rather subversive thrill to be had sitting in a seat that stands starkly outside of its natural habitat (the interior of a Rover 2000). There's a delight, too, in a stationary chair that effortlessly conjures up images of speeding along roads with the wind in your hair. The Rover chair was not, however, an example of Arad sticking two fingers up at the grand traditions of furniture design. Indeed, it can be perceived as doing quite the opposite. 'I just noticed there was so much design and engineering and craftsmanship in this leather car seat,' Arad once said in a recorded conversation with the artist Matthew Collings, 'and you'd see hundreds of them rotting in scrap yards, and they're more comfortable than any chair you can buy.' Why design a new chair, he seems to have been saying, when there are such very good ones out there already? However, Arad's provocative design was not immediately appreciated. A single Rover chair sat in the corner of his studio for over a year until, on Boxing Day in 1981, the fashion designer Jean Paul Gaultier bought six of them, for £99 each. After that, as Arad says, 'people couldn't get enough of Rover chairs'.

The first chair was a red leather Rover seat on a tubular-steel frame. 'I made the frame,' says Arad, 'which was a semicircle, and I put together the things that needed to be put together, and it was right first time … It didn't need to be improved.' The scaffolding-like appearance of the base was a wilfully crude take on the then-popular High Tech style – perhaps best showcased by the Pompidou Centre in Paris, designed by Richard Rogers and Renzo Piano.

Ironically, having picked up a pair of seats from a scrap yard in north London, Arad had no idea that those first red leather seats were, in fact, something of a rarity. Produced by Arad from 1981 until 1991, nearly all of the subsequent Rover chairs had the far more commonplace black seats … and the laws of supply and demand, rarity and desirability, have subsequently applied: a red leather Rover chair at auction today will today fetch far more than a black one.

Left and above
The Rover is mounted on a High Tech style, scaffolding-like tubular-steel frame, and retains its original lever-operated adjustable back rest.

How High the Moon / 1986

If ever a piece of furniture could be described as poetic it is surely this one. Given the lyrical name of 'How High the Moon' applied by its designer, Shiro Kuramata (1934–91), the chair creates a visual paradox. We see that it is bulky in form, yet it appears so light in weight as to be almost floating. And while the luxurious proportions speak of comfort and prosperity, the steel mesh suggests the opposite.

Kuramata's playful approach to furniture design was developed over a relatively long period, and he was in his fifties when he began to make an international name for himself. Before this he had worked as an architect, an ad man and a traditional cabinet-maker. By the 1980s his distinctive style was honed to such a point that he managed to produce designs for furniture and interiors in prolific numbers, but with an astonishing consistency in quality.

Often described as Post-Modern, Kuramata's designs display a lightness of touch not usually associated with this cerebral movement. His work utilizes industrial materials (such as steel mesh or plastic), while employing them in a delicate way.

Although made from an inexpensive material, How High the Moon is a relatively pricey piece to manufacture. Made by Vitra, it involves considerable skill and time, especially with the crispness of finish demanded by Kuramata. The chair's deceptively simple appearance is created by soldering together 17 pieces of steel mesh and hanging them on a steel matrix, which means that there are more than 2,300 points that require soldering before the piece is complete. The resulting form is then tuned to eliminate twisting and finally plated with nickel and coated with epoxy resin.

How High the Moon is, therefore, something of a technical feat, yet the arduous nature of the production process is not apparent in the final feather-light form. While some have criticized Kuramata for what they perceive as the use of deception in design, most admire such sleight of hand. Indeed, Kuramata was instrumental in raising the profile of furniture design to a level where it could stand shoulder to shoulder with art, and this trend for 'design art', as it is sometimes called, has resulted in conceptually driven furniture design attracting huge sums at auctions alongside cutting-edge contemporary art.

Above
Reminiscent of pale, glowing moonlight, the shimmering metal surface prompted Kuramata to borrow the chair's name from Duke Ellington's song 'How High the Moon'.

Embryo / 1988

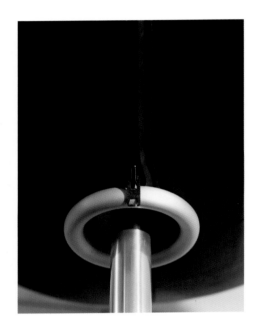

Marc Newson's Embryo chair was, in more ways than one, aptly named. Not only does the title describe its primal shape, but the chair also had a considerable influence on a brasher and more playful style that became prevalent in international design during the following decade: the 1990s.

The 25-year-old Newson (b. 1963) designed the chair in Sydney, Australia, where he lived in a seafront hotel run by his mother. It is not difficult to make the link between Newson's design and the Australian city's vibrant surf culture – especially when you see the wetsuit fabric that covers the chair. 'For me the chair represented something very optimistic,' Newson has said, 'It showed the future.'

Newson's laid-back and upbeat approach to design was noticeably at odds with that of European designers, most of whom at the time were in the thick of the heavy, theory-based movement Post-Modernism. The simple biomorphic shape of the Embryo, whether in black, as pictured here, or in bright primary colours (which Newson described as 'very Australian'), was a breath of fresh air.

Newson was determinedly against the rigidity of the straight line – he preferred curves – and was not afraid of using outrageous colour. 'This was one of the first pieces where I hit upon a discernible style,' he later explained. It was a style that soon propelled him to the very forefront of the international design scene. Indeed, so acclaimed did he become that he left Australia, a relatively minor player in the international design industry, and took up residence first in Tokyo, then in Paris and finally in London, as his career sky-rocketed.

Moving to England was a natural move for Newson, as the 'discernible style' that he defined with the Embryo chair was not only inspired by Australian beach culture, he was also indebted to the ultimate Englishman, James Bond. The Bond filmsets, with the villains' futuristic lairs, had enthralled Newson as a young boy, and he had no intention of growing out of this passion as an adult designer. Add to that his enthusiasm for Bond's Aston Martin cars (one of which he soon bought himself following the Embryo's instant success), and one can see why he settled in England's capital city.

The Embryo chair, which is composed of a neoprene-covered polyurethane foam seat on a tubular-steel frame, is still in production, being manufactured by Idée in Japan (where Newson has a big fan base) and Cappellini in Italy. Although Newson has now moved on to designing cars and the interiors of aircraft, it was this remarkable chair that proved to be the launch pad for the Australian's glittering career.

Above
In homage to Australia's surfing culture, Embryo's bi-elastic cover is zipped at the back like a wetsuit.

Favela / 1991

Against a background of a global society dominated by technology, the launch of the ramshackle Favela chair by the Brazilian brothers Humberto and Fernando Campana proved a thrilling sight. Although originally designed in 1991, the chair had not been much seen beyond the pair's São Paulo studio until it wowed the crowds with its wilful primitivism at the European design fairs in 2003.

'I saw a bunch of slats on the street in front of my studio,' Humberto Campana told the US magazine *Metropolis*, 'and I thought to myself, "Why don't you clean them and make a chair like people construct in a favela?"' Favela is a term used to describe shantytowns – areas of South American cities where people live in extreme poverty, typically in homes crudely constructed from random pieces of found materials. Usually these homes have furniture inside them fashioned in a similar manner.

This spirit of 'make do and mend' has always inspired the Campanas, and the Favela is perhaps the purest expression of this interest. Other furniture pieces by the brothers make use of overlooked materials such as bubble wrap, string, cardboard and even garden hose, but many of these lack the lyrical beauty of the Favela. It is the beguiling patterns formed by the chair's construction, and the exhilaration of such a sturdy object being formed from tiny scraps of wood, that make this an outstanding design.

Although the chair is produced by the Italian manufacturer Edra, it is entirely made by hand in Brazil. Carpenters nail and glue pieces of wood onto a frame to build up chairs that each have their own unique appearance. The chair is, clearly, something of a retort to the slick industrialism of many European furniture manufacturers, from a design duo who know that beauty lies in the unlikeliest of places.

Although now fêted in the United States and Europe, where companies are queuing up to put Campana designs into production, the brothers refuse to relocate from their native city of São Paulo. 'Brazil is our great fountain of inspiration,' they say, insisting that 'the designer of the future must use references from his cultural background so that his products have an authenticity and originality that is not governed by fashion or global trends'.

By resolutely ploughing their own path, the Campanas have built up a firm international following – something that the pair admit that they did not envision when they formed a partnership in 1983. Considering that neither had any training in furniture design (Fernando trained as an architect, while Humberto was a lawyer) and that São Paulo hardly figured on the global design map before the Campanas, it is most certainly a remarkable achievement.

Above
Gluing and nailing together all the pieces of wood by hand means that no two Favelas are exactly the same.

Balzac / 1991

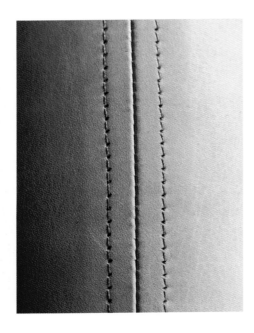

The curvaceous shape of Matthew Hilton's Balzac chair instantly communicates that comfort is what this design is all about. Its long, laid-back profile – especially when augmented with a matching ottoman – speaks of lazy evenings with a good book and a glass of wine. Indeed, Hilton (b. 1957) consciously designed the Balzac as an update of the classic club chair, a seating type that originated in the private gentlemen's clubs of Victorian England. Men would go to these clubs seeking rest and relaxation, an enduring and universal urge that has turned the accommodating Balzac into a bestseller.

Hilton has said, 'The shape and position of the chair come from where I felt one's body would want to be,' and thus the ergonomic design was created by drawing around bodies reclining on makeshift seats made from piles of books – the seats being altered and adjusted until Hilton found what he thought was the optimum form. The soft outline of the chair was also deliberately sculptural. Hilton had originally planned to become an artist before he turned his attention to design, and much of his inspiration for the chair came not from other pieces of furniture, but from artworks. It is Hilton's belief that looking at too much design provokes a tendency to follow trends, diluting true function and originality. The Balzac, which is both wonderfully functional and original, surely bears out this belief.

The chair has a beech frame with steel springs and elasticated webbing covered with foam and feather cushions. The legs are made of oak, and the covering is most commonly leather (although other fabrics are available). The Balzac was the first upholstered chair that Hilton had designed, although his inexperience in no way hindered its success. It was commissioned by SCP, the pioneering British manufacturing company formed by Sheridan Coakley (after whose dog the chair is named). SCP was a key force in reviving international interest in British design in the latter years of the 20th century, and the Balzac was one of the most important components of the SCP range. 'At the time, people abroad thought the British only had antique furniture,' says Hilton, as he remembers travelling across the world representing SCP.

When it was launched at the Paris Furniture Fair, the Balzac design received its first order from design guru and home furnishings retail magnate Terence Conran. Singing its praises as the best piece of furniture he'd seen for years, he was soon stocking it in his shops across the world. This kick-started the ongoing success of a design that is frequently spotted nowadays not only in residential interiors and the odd gentlemen's club, but also in upmarket hotel lobbies and airport lounges the world over.

Above left
As befits its gentlemen's club origins, the Balzac's foam and feather upholstery is usually covered in a traditionally stitched aniline hide.

Lord Yo / 1994

Parisian-born Philippe Starck (b. 1949) describes himself as a 'product designer', and it is not difficult to understand why. The Lord Yo chair is but one from a prolific and diverse output of products that have influenced just about every sphere of the design world. From buildings, interiors, furniture and kitchen utensils to yachts, Starck's designs are everywhere. So, what makes the Lord Yo stand out? What makes it special?

Although designed in 1994, it is essentially a classic tub chair. Indeed, its overall shape is highly reminiscent of a Lloyd Loom lounge chair from the 1930s (see page 179). As with Starck's subsequent re-interpretation, in 2002, of an 18th-century Louis XVI chair (see the Louis Ghost on page 306), this rather begs the question, why should the reworking of a traditional and already well-known chair be applauded as good, even great, design? On a fundamental level the Lord Yo does exactly what it is meant to. The rigid polypropylene and aluminium construction not only lends itself to three of Starck's design ideals – mass production, affordability and therefore mass consumption – but also makes it suitable for indoor or outdoor use, and for the office or the home. Indeed, the fact that it stacks (up to four chairs high) also makes it an excellent restaurant or café chair.

Starck has sometimes been criticized for paring down and reducing interiors to rather bleak, stark spaces. With Lord Yo, however, there are options. First, the polypropylene shell is available from the manufacturer Driade in different colours: apricot, red, grey-blue, white and, as here, ivory. Secondly, the availability of loose fabric or leather covers – in white, grey-green or blue – allows the chair to be 'softened up' for more lush or traditional interiors, or for different functions, such as 'on' when dining, and 'off' when not. Moreover, this adaptability can be further enhanced with the use of various loose seat cushions.

In fact, the Lord Yo is very comfortable in its unadorned 'bare-bones' form, with much of this the result of a particularly supportive high back, slightly splayed arms, and a front skirt or apron that cushions the backs of the occupant's knees. Ultimately, however, Lord Yo's desirability resides beyond comfort and in the elegant simplicity of its form. Indeed, viewed without a sitter, appealing anthropomorphic qualities become readily apparent, perhaps recalling, very appropriately, the serene and majestic posture of a seated Samurai lord in an Akira Kurosawa epic.

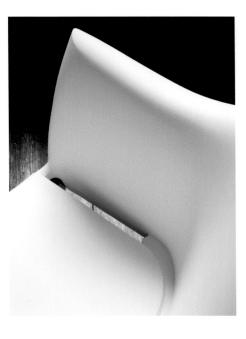

Right
A rigid polypropylene shell makes Lord Yo suitable for indoor and outdoor use.

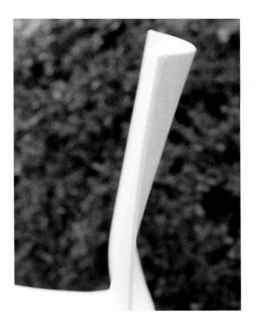

The Bellini Chair / 1998

Conceived by the Italian architect and designer Mario Bellini (b. 1935) and made by the furniture manufacturer Heller, the Bellini chair has, since its launch in 1998, been the recipient of numerous design awards, including Italy's prestigious Compasso d'Oro. Other impressive endorsements have included being chosen as the café chair for New York's Museum of Modern Art and inclusion in the New York Metropolitan Museum of Art's collection of modern design. *Interni* magazine went so far as to describe it as 'one of the most intelligent chairs in the world … a truly universal chair'. So what is it about the Bellini chair that has provoked such lavish praise?

Functionality plays a big part. Its fibreglass-reinforced polypropylene body stands up to heavy use in domestic or commercial environments, indoors and out, and is easy to scrub clean. The lightly textured matt finish, which on close inspection resembles leather, plays a subtle supportive role – unlike some plastic chairs, there is little danger of sliding off a Bellini. Similarly, the legs are provided with foot pads to stop slippage on hard floors and to protect the floor from scuffing. Weighing in at just under 3.5kg (7 1/2 lb), the chair is easy to move around and can be stacked up to six high when not in use.

In addition, Milan-born Mario Bellini, who was a key figure in the revitalization of Italian design during the 1970s, was able to incorporate an exceptionally high level of comfort. This is provided by combining a gently concave seat with a similarly profiled back, which, by slightly flexing as the sitter leans back or forwards, is very supportive of the spine.

Comfort is an essential ingredient, but the appearance of the chair is what has really ensured its status as an instant classic. The fact that it seems to sit just as happily in an office, a restaurant or a home can be partly attributed to the availability of different colours to suit different schemes. Black, dark grey, light grey, sage, white and, as here, cream – all in a matt finish – were in 2007 augmented by high-gloss white, black, 'red red' and 'blue blue' in a spin-off model, the UltraBellini chair. Ultimately, however, it is the fluid, seemingly simple but elegant proportions of the Bellini that underpin its desirability. Indeed, as designer Terence Conran commented in a 1999 *New York Times* interview about the Bellini, 'For $80 you can have a piece of sculpture in your home.'

Right
The gently concave seat and similarly profiled back offer the sitter a high level of comfort.

Louis Ghost / 2002

The world's first totally transparent polycarbonate chair was La Marie, designed in 1997 by Philippe Starck (b. 1949). The technical experimentation that resulted in the advent of this see-through chair was a painstaking and difficult journey, involving highly intensive research, but, once resolved, it allowed Starck and the manufacturer Kartell to progress with more sophisticated forms – most notably the Louis Ghost of 2002.

Starck called it the Louis Ghost because the design of the chair is based on a French Louis XVI form – a classic style in its own right. Certainly, the elegance of the original was never in doubt, but what is one to think of such a blatantly 'plagiarized' form? Such revisits always have their critics, but there is a braveness in attempting to re-interpret a classic historical form – and in this case it works admirably, albeit with a large dose of humorous irony: this is 18th-century Neo-Classicism revisited in an intangible, 'ghostly' polycarbonate form.

It would be fair to say that not all of Starck's designs have hit all the right notes. For example, his famous Juicy Salif lemon squeezer, designed for Alessi in 1990, has become an affordable cult classic. It looks fantastic, but it is messy to use – proof that form over function can sometimes prevail. The Louis Ghost, however, has few such issues. Like most of Starck's designs, it is extremely versatile. It stacks six-high, it can be used indoors or outdoors, it is durable and it is scratch-resistant. Moreover, its mood can change to suit different environments. Subtly altered with a palette of colours, batch-tinted in transparent tones, or even rich opaque jet black, it has a chameleon-like quality. Kartell also offers a quirky personalization service for the chair, with four basic decorative transfers centrally applied to the back panel and based on facially related themes; if this doesn't fulfil your remit, then it is also possible to order your own design, but only for a minimum of 50!

So, from good beginnings come great things, and the progression from La Marie to the Louis Ghost has spawned a whole family of Ghost chairs. The Lou Lou Ghost is the child's version, the Victoria Ghost is Victorian, while the Charles Ghost is simply billed as an indestructible polycarbonate stool. The enduring success of the Louis and its siblings may partly depend on the ironic humour inherent in the design, but ultimately it will be guaranteed by the recognition that this ghost is a shadow from the past very cleverly re-presented and preserved for the future.

Chair_One / 2004

Konstantin Grcic's Chair_One has become one of the defining chairs of the early years of the 21st century, thanks to its combination of industrial rigour and aesthetic charm. Designed by the Munich-based designer Grcic (b. 1965) in response to a request from Magis, the Italian furniture manufacturer, to produce a chair using the technique of aluminium casting, the chair took four years to develop before finally going on sale in 2004.

The lattice structure of the seat lends the chair a lightness of form that counterbalances the more rough-and-ready nature of the materials used. It is, as Grcic says, 'a truly industrial chair', but it also has an expressive, individualistic quality that identifies its designer not as an out-and-out Modernist, but as someone with a more contemporary, subversive spirit. When Grcic talks about the 'surprisingly high level of comfort' that the chair affords, we can see that function was not the driving force of the form, but a welcome though unexpected by-product. In his work, Grcic fluidly combines the languages of both art and industry. The creative process that produced Chair_One is a testament to the Grcic's dexterity as a designer. While the chair is obviously the conception of an independent mind, its development involved a whole raft of different technicians, assistants and consultants. While the initial forms of the chair were created by Grcic bending, and tinkering with, a single stretch of wire ('like a three-dimensional drawing', as he describes it), the final shape was honed using the highly complex programs of a computer.

Key figures involved in the production of Chair_One, other than Grcic himself, include Benoit Steenackers of the Magis technical office, Gianni Zin of the Zin Group (a company specializing in the engineering and manufacture of moulds for aluminium die-casting), a group of structural engineers from the company Area 3 and, perhaps most importantly, Stefan Diez, who was then Grcic's assistant, but has since gone on to establish himself as a renowned furniture designer in his own right. The chair, then, is a result of four years of Italian–German collaboration. Indeed, many of the meetings that took place over that time were held in a service station halfway between Munich (Grcic's hometown) and Motta di Livenza (the Italian town where Magis has its headquarters).

The success of Chair_One has prompted production of it in various guises, from the simple stacking chair to bench-like beam seating. All employ the same web-like seat, but on a variety of different bases, from cast concrete, as here, to splayed steel legs. The design has even spawned offspring such as a table and stool. It is however, the chair and that web-like aluminium seat that will endure as the classic form and component of the design.

Above
Grcic has described Chair_One as being 'constructed like a football: a number of flat planes assembled at angles to each other, creating the three-dimensional form'.

Lazy Seating 05 – High Back / 2004–5

The prototype for this high-back chair was designed in 2004 by the Spanish-born architect and designer Patricia Urquiola (b. 1961). Together with a chaise longue, a low-back, an easy chair, an armchair and a stool – collectively known as Lazy Seating 05 – it was put into production in 2005 by B&B Italia. Given its pedigree, the Lazy's subsequent commercial success was perhaps inevitable. Fostered by the eminent Italian designers Achille Castiglioni, under whom she studied, and Vico Magistretti, Urquiola has become one of the great new stars of the design world. Fuelled by a seemingly boundless creative energy, her already substantial and diverse portfolio includes projects not only for B&B, but also for many other prestigious furniture manufacturers, notably Cappellini, Cassina, Kartell and Knoll. Not surprisingly, all this has seen her hailed in some quarters as the 'female Philippe Starck'.

Such provenance is certainly desirable, but the appeal of the Lazy High-Back ultimately lies in its impressive qualities of form, style and indeed comfort. The nuts and bolts of the design are a slender tubular-shaped steel frame with a chrome finish; a thermoformed plastic under polyurethane and polyester fibre seat; a polyester fibre over webbing back rest; and woven fibre or leather top covers available in various colours (including two-tone). Together they present a chair that, despite its outward simplicity, challenges you to find a familiar form or association.

Viewed head-on, its high back seems reminiscent of a seated Pharaoh – so the chair is perhaps a little magisterial and aloof, yet it manages to appear at the same time soft and welcoming. It also exudes a positive feeling, an upbeat presence, which is in fact characteristic of Urquiola's furniture designs.

Seen from the side, the Lazy High-Back displays a fluidity of form that successfully mixes hard angles with soft curves. Again, this is typical of Urquiola's work. Her lush sofa and chair designs for the Italian furniture manufacturer Moroso peddle a similarly sumptuous simplicity, drawing you into a comfortable world of underlying luxury and femininity – the latter a quality often absent from the world of cold, crisp high-end design. Perhaps that hint of femininity is subconscious, hovering just below the surface. In a field that is largely male-dominated, Urquiola has infiltrated the masculine ranks of design and imbued it with a new kind of optimism and balance.

In some respects, the Lazy High-Back sports a misnomer: although it invites us into a world of relaxation and comfort, it is far from passive itself. Highly proactive, it invariably enhances living spaces and work spaces alike with its form, its colour and its characteristically Urquiola panache.

Above and left
The Lazy High-Back's slender but strong chromed-steel frame and its body-conforming upholstery provide elegant, resilient and comfortable seating.

Poltrona Suave / 2005

Julia Krantz is an emerging Brazilian designer with considerable talent. In its scale, relationship to sustainable design, craftsmanship and understanding of materials, the Poltrona Suave (meaning 'smooth armchair') encapsulates all of the qualities that make her furniture so exceptional.

One of the first things that strikes you is the scale of the chair, which corresponds to the designer's aspirations. The piece has a presence – it is not diminutive, and neither is Krantz's mission to make extraordinary sculptural furniture without compromising her commitment to ecological sustainability. All of her works are created using only timbers obtained through sustainable management.

The Poltrona Moleca, like her other furniture, is created in Krantz's studio starting from a mould. For the next step – which for many contemporary designers would involve a computer-generated prototype – she opts for the handmade, imbuing the chair with a softness not possible from a machine. This process involves stack-laminating the wood by hand, then smoothing and carving the surface by hand, resulting in subtle curves and details that correspond to the ways in which people will sit in the chair. One of the most impressive consequences of this is a wooden chair with the comfort of an upholstered lounge chair. This time-consuming, almost obsessive interaction with the material also results in a wonderfully animated quality. In particular, the strident patterns of figuring formed by the stack-laminating technique create a sense of motion that infuses the chair with a vibrant energy.

Ultimately, the Poltrana Suave is a sculpture in wood. Made in limited editions employed different coloured woods – some chairs are lighter, some darker – the ultra-thin wooden laminates have been manipulated into sensuous, curvaceous waves, then polished to an inviting smoothness. It is impossible not to touch the chair, to run your hands over the curves, to be enveloped by its sensuousness. Krantz has remarked, 'A friend of mine says that my designs take the form of falling water. I never would have thought of such an image, but I think it fits.' It does indeed: to sit in her chair is in some ways to sink luxuriously back into the water while being held safely above the lapping waves.

Transfigure / 2006

With its look of an organic sculpture, its laminated-wood construction and its intrinsic functionality, Transfigure, by Wendell Castle (b. 1932), bears all the hallmarks of its designer's most important contributions to the history of American furniture design. In 1959, while still a student at the University of Kansas, Castle challenged his professors, and the age-old divisions between furniture and art, by entering a piece entitled 'Stool Sculpture' into a juried art exhibition. This episode foreshadowed half a century of work in which Castle has defied both categorization and traditional furniture-making techniques, to pursue the freedom of thought and execution inherent in the sculptor's language. In doing so he has galvanized an entire generation of designers and inspired the American studio furniture movement, in which the conceptual and the aesthetic are judged as important to the success of a piece as its functionality.

Castle's signature technique is stack-lamination, in which boards are glued together and clamped until they form a unified whole and are then carved, sanded and detailed. The technique was originally inspired by Leonard Baskin (1922–2000), a sculptor who glued together small wood blocks into a large aggregate, then carved the whole into the desired shape. Castle realized he could use the same additive process, but pre-shape the boards and fashion the wedges only as large as they needed to be, thereby saving a huge amount of wood and creating his own precise working method. Moreover, this technique could be used to forge pieces that were much bigger and, if he staggered the built-up boards, more binding than a large rectangular block. 'It was a way to make furniture without knowing how to make furniture,' he recalled.

Subsequently, Castle developed both an immaculate technical virtuosity and a distinct and overriding aesthetic, often incorporating organic forms. As he explained, 'To me an organic form has the most exciting possibilities. An organic form is not so clearly understood in one glance.'

In 2006, with Transfigure, Castle created a work of art that is as complex in concept as it is in its layering. Stemming from an organic pedestal-type base, the abstract carved shell seat both coddles and presents its sitter. The base, simulating a mound of earth, seems autonomous despite being linked to the seat by its sprouting 'stem'. The contrast continues with the controlled tool marks on the laminated base, juxtaposed with the smoothness of the seat, which renders the construction technique transparent, as evidenced through the relatively light colour of the wood. 'Flawlessly' constructed, the chair could even be viewed as touching on the spiritual. Indeed, Castle himself hinted — albeit in a suitably understated way — at such a conceptual aspect when he noted that 'the title of Transfigure refers to the transformation of the piece from a pile of boards into something more important'.

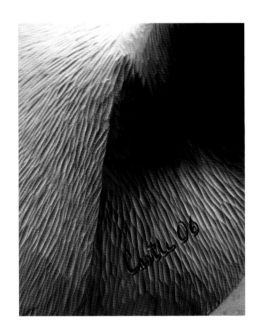

Above
Transfigure's shell seat and signed pedestal base are fashioned from oil-finished laminated mahogany, but while the seat is rendered smooth the base is textured with hand-tooling.

'Wingback' / 2007

Tom Dixon's theatrical design for the Wingback chair brings a flamboyant drama to the humble activity of sitting down. The towering, curvaceous back and seductive mohair velvet upholstery make this chair more a contemporary throne than a mere place to park your backside. Of course, the roots of this design go back not to royal palaces, but to the privileged living rooms of the late 17th and 18th centuries, where wingback chairs were a common sight. Tom Dixon (b. 1959) himself openly admits that his is not a new design idea, but rather the updating of an old one. 'How many shapes do we need a chair to be?' he once argued, suggesting that all the best seating forms had already been found.

Considering that the Wingback is based on chairs with which most of us are familiar, it is a testament to Dixon's design skills that it is still such a startling sight. Perhaps the perversely exaggerated shape of the chair – with its miniature legs and long, arching back – is what makes it so curious. Cleverly, however, the slick craftsmanship and obvious sophistication of the construction ensure that this chair stays just the right side of becoming a comic novelty.

The Wingback is made using centuries-old techniques and in many ways is a nostalgic throwback to a time before industrial furniture factories. When it was launched in 2007, great play was made of the painstaking construction of the wooden frame and the feather and velvet upholstery by displaying the chair in various stages of production. Such a time-consuming process adds up to a chair that is not cheap: prices for purchasing a Wingback in the year of its launch were a substantial £3,600.

As a designer, Tom Dixon has always been keen on the idea of recycling – be it of materials or, in the case of the Wingback, ideas. In the early days of his career, he constructed furniture from industrial scrap under the banner of Creative Salvage, a company he formed with the designer Mark Brazier-Jones. Both Brazier-Jones and Dixon had backgrounds in the music and fashion business, rather than formal design educations, so their approach to design was more carefree than many of their contemporaries. This pleasingly dilettante approach, where the traditions of designs are neither railed against nor revered, but rather just joyously plundered, pervades all of Dixon's work. While the Wingback might not win any awards for innovation, its sheer charm will surely ensure a lasting reputation.

New Gaudi / 2007

This is the last chair designed by the influential Italian architect and designer Vico Magistretti (1920–2006). Made by international furniture manufacturer Heller and launched a year after Magistretti's death in 2006, it encapsulates the inspired marriage of design and technology that underpinned Magistretti's work, and especially his ground-breaking use of plastics dating back to the 1960s.

In a 2000 interview with the ezine *designboom* Magistretti said, 'I never like to go back to work I've already completed … [it's] sort of like how the guilty person should never go back to the scene of the crime.' Subsequently, he obviously thought better of it, because New Gaudi is Magistretti's reworking of the Gaudi armchair he designed in 1970. Manufactured for three years by Artemide, the original design was broader than its more upright offspring and, being compression-moulded from fibreglass-reinforced polyester, was heavier, too. The New Gaudi is one-piece injection-moulded from a more scientifically advanced polymer, making it not only lighter, but also stronger. Other changes include different colour choices (white, black or grey, rather than the white, grey, dark brown or green of the originals) and the dropping of the old high-gloss finish in favour of a softer, silkier matt look.

Over the years, the original Gaudi had developed something of a cult following, a phenomenon partly fuelled by its prominent appearance in the hit TV series *Space 1999* during the mid-1970s. It is simply too early to know for sure whether the slimmer New Gaudi will acquire similar iconic status, but the portents are favourable. First, it retains the original's sculptural elegance. Enhanced by seamless, one-piece moulding, this is a characteristic of Magistretti's designs, and one that back in the late 1960s helped to elevate the status of plastic to a material appropriate for fine furniture.

The new chair also retains the original's technical sophistication, the most impressive feature of which is Magistretti's innovative design for the legs. Because they are folded lengthwise, to form a U-profile along the front and a corresponding S-profile at the back, they are able to withstand considerable tensile stress and are therefore highly resistant to buckling. Typically, their configuration also contributes to the graceful fluidity of the overall design.

Another admirable feature is the perforations at the inner corners of the seat, a technical necessity imposed by integrating the arms within a one-piece construction. If the chair is kept outside and caught in the rain, the perforations help rainwater to drain off and the seat to stay dry. Ultimately, however, the appeal of the perforations is as much aesthetic as functional, which is entirely appropriate in a chair designed by Magistretti. Inspired by Modernist ideals, he always sought to produce simple, functional, rational and elegant designs – and has certainly succeeded here.

Nirvana / 2007

Futuristic, with slick surfaces and supple melding forms, the extraordinary Nirvana is perhaps more reminiscent of a spacecraft than a chair. Although very much a 21st-century conception by Wendell Castle (b. 1932), it pays homage the American designer's explorations in plastics back in the 1960s and 1970s, while being testament to his artistic and technical development during the intervening decades.

By the late 1960s, Castle was already renowned for marrying art and design through his sculptor's approach to furniture-making and his technique of stack-laminating wood (see page 317). At that time the acknowledged master of wood, he sought to challenge himself with new materials and simultaneously broaden his audience by making a more affordable product. Thus in 1969–70 he issued his Molar Group, in which furniture shaped like human teeth was made of what looked like candy – shimmering gel-coated fibreglass-reinforced plastic. With an American public enamoured of Pop Art at the time, Castle's wave-like silhouettes, fantasy forms and vibrant hues proved an instant success.

Although influenced by 1930s Surrealism (Salvador Dali's sofa in the shape of Mae West's lips, for example) and post-war Italian design, Castle's forms were and are ultimately his own. Moreover, plastics and fibreglass have enabled him to translate the feeling of movement that he has achieved when stacking and clamping wood laminates into even more exuberant, unfettered shapes. With Nirvana he was also able to harness years of research into fibreglass paint colours and finishes, together with more efficient techniques of mould-making.

Key Castle signatures such as asymmetry, biomorphism, cone legs and aquatic fins can be seen in Nirvana. The chair's functional elements, such as the built-in table surface to one side and the generously rounded seat, are also consistent with his other work. Nirvana's colour, however, is very much a contemporary finesse: several coats of automobile-grade metal-flake urethane paint, the type favoured by hot-rod restorers, have been applied to the surface. This has created an almost ineffable iridescence that subtly graduates from blue to purple to aubergine (eggplant), depending on the light and one's standpoint. It is also consolidates the remarkable unity of form Castle has achieved using innovative multiple-component moulds – a technical advance that has made most shapes possible without compromising structural integrity. This bodes well: with virtually no technical restrictions on form, Castle can continue to push his sculptural vocabulary beyond the envelope. Indeed, as he himself has said, 'With fibreglass, the possibilities are virtually limitless.'

Acknowledgements

PAGE 32
Wainscot Armchair | c.1640
Witney Antiques

PAGE 34
Banister-Back Armchair | c.1700–10
Bernard & S. Dean Levy, Inc.

PAGE 36
Daniel Marot-style Side Chair |
c.1710
Witney Antiques

PAGE 40
Queen Anne Open Armchair |
c.1710
Partridge Fine Arts Ltd

PAGE 42
Régence *Fauteuil* | c.1720
Partridge Fine Arts Ltd

PAGE 46
American Queen Anne Wing
Chair | c.1745
Bernard & S. Dean Levy, Inc.

PAGE 48
American Queen Anne Side
Chair | c.1750
Bernard & S. Dean Levy, Inc.

PAGE 50
Louis XV *Fauteuil* | c.1755
Partridge Fine Arts Ltd

PAGE 52
George II Open Armchair | c.1755
John Bly Antiques

PAGE 56
American Chippendale Rococo
Side Chair | c.1765
Bernard & S. Dean Levy, Inc.

PAGE 58
American Chippendale Gothic
Side Chair | c.1775
Bernard & S. Dean Levy, Inc.

PAGE 60
Chinese Chippendale 'Cockpen' |
c.1775
Partridge Fine Arts Ltd

PAGE 62
George III Faux Bamboo Open
Armchair | c.1775
Partridge Fine Arts Ltd

PAGE 64
Windsor Comb-Back | c.1775
John Bly Antiques

PAGE 68
Country Ladderback | c.1780
Judith Miller & John Wainwright

PAGE 70
George III Tub Chair | c.1780
Partridge Fine Arts Ltd

PAGE 72
George III Polychrome-painted
Shield-Back | c.1785
Partridge Fine Arts Ltd

PAGE 74
George III Louis XVI-style Open
Armchair | c.1790
Partridge Fine Arts Ltd

PAGE 78
Regency Dining Chair | c.1805
John Bly Antiques

PAGE 80
American Federal Armchair | c.1805
Bernard & S. Dean Levy, Inc.

PAGE 82
Regency Gothic Side Chair | c.1810
Partridge Fine Arts Ltd

PAGE 84
Regency Chaise Longue | c.1810
Partridge Fine Arts Ltd

PAGE 88
Regency 'Grecian-Egyptian'
Armchair | c.1815
Partridge Fine Arts Ltd

PAGE 90
Regency 'Egyptian-Grecian'
Armchair | c.1815
Witney Antiques

PAGE 94
'Sheraton-Grecian' Dining Chair |
c.1820
Partridge Fine Arts Ltd

PAGE 96
French Restauration *Fauteuil* | c.1820
Partridge Fine Arts Ltd

PAGE 98
Victorian Hall Chair | c.1860
Partridge Fine Arts Ltd

PAGE 100
Victorian Feather-Back | 1860s
Judith Miller & John Wainwright

PAGE 102
Victorian Chaise Longue | 1860s
Claire Veillard and John Cornwell

PAGE 106
Arts & Crafts Ladderback | c.1870
Terence Conran

PAGE 108
Victorian Queen Anne Revival
Side Chair | 1880s
Partridge Fine Arts Ltd

PAGE 110
Sheraton-Revival Corner Chair |
c.1890–1910
Judith Miller & John Wainwright

PAGE 112
Historical-Revival Wing Chair |
c.1890–1910
John Bly Antiques

The publisher would like to thank the following photographers and agencies for their kind permission to reproduce the following photographs:

PAGE 10 | TopFoto
PAGE 12 TOP | The Trustees of the British Museum
PAGE 12 BOTTOM | J Paul Getty Museum
PAGE 13 | Scala, Florence/ Fotografica Foglia, Courtesy of the Ministero Beni e Att. Culturali
PAGE 14 | Private Collection/ Ken Walsh/ The Bridgeman Art Library
PAGE 15 | Millers/Lyon & Turnbull Ltd
PAGE 16 TOP | V & A Images, Victoria and Albert Museum
PAGE 16 BOTTOM | Scala, Florence (1990)
PAGE 17 TOP | Millers/Dreweatt's
PAGE 17 BOTTOM | Millers/ Partridge Fine Arts plc
PAGE 18 | Millers/Northeast Auctions
PAGE 19 TOP | Philadelphia Museum of Art: Gift of the McNeil Americana Collection, 1991. Ph: Graydon Wood
PAGE 19 BOTTOM | Millers/ Bukowskis
PAGE 20 | Philadelphia Museum of Art: Bequest of Fiske & Marie Kimball, 1955. Ph: Graydon Wood
PAGE 21 TOP | Philadelphia Museum of Art: Purchased with the gift (by exchange) of Mrs Alex Simpson, Jr., & A. Carson Simpson, and with

funds contributed by Mr & Mrs Robert L. Raley & various donors, 1986. Ph: Graydon Wood
PAGE 21 BOTTOM | Millers/Bukowskis
PAGE 22 TOP | Nina Leen/Time Life Pictures/Getty Images
PAGE 22 BOTTOM | Millers/ Quittenbaum
PAGE 23 TOP | Millers/Woolley & Wallis
PAGE 23 BOTTOM | Cheltenham Art Gallery & Museums, Gloucestershire UK/ The Bridgeman Art Library
PAGE 24 TOP | Millers/Rago Arts
PAGE 24 BOTTOM | Millers/ Palais Dorotheum
PAGE 25 TOP | Millers/Jazzy Art Deco
PAGE 25 BOTTOM | Millers/Palais Dorotheum
PAGE 26 TOP | Millers/Palais Dorotheum
PAGE 26 BOTTOM | Millers/Bonhams
PAGE 27 TOP | Millers/Bonhams
PAGE 27 BOTTOM | Courtesy of Studio d'Urbino Lomazzi
PAGE 28 TOP | Courtesy of Gaetano Pesce
PAGE 28 BOTTOM | Millers/Quittenbaum
PAGE 29 | Edra

Every effort has been made to trace the copyright holders. We apologize in advance for any unintentional omissions and would be pleased to insert the appropriate acknowledgement in any subsequent publication.

Stockists

Alivar
www.alivar.it

Amat-3
www.amat-3.com

Aram
110 Drury Lane
London WC2B 5SG
UK
Tel. +44 (0)20 7557 7557
www.aram.co.uk

Artek
www.artek.fi

B&B Italia
www.bebitalia.it

BD Barcelona
www.bdbarcelona.com

Bernard & S. Dean Levy, Inc.
24 East 84th Street
New York, NY 10028
USA
Tel. +1 (212) 628 7088
E-mail:
American@LevyGalleries.com
www.levygalleries.com

John Bly Antiques
The Courtyard, Church Square
Tring, Hertfordshire HP23 5AE
UK
Tel. +44 (0)1442 823 030
Also by appointment at:
27 Bury Street
London SW1Y 6AL
UK
Tel. +44 (0)7831 888 825/6
E-mail: john@johnbly.com
www.johnbly.com

The Cale Schiang Partnership
58 Holywell Hill, St Albans
Hertfordshire AL1 1BX
UK
Tel. +44 (0)8702 202055
www.schiang.com

Conran Shop
www.conranshop.co.uk

Domus Gallery
15 Needham Road
London W11 2RP
UK
Tel. +44 (0)20 7221 1666
www.domusgallery.co.uk

Driade
www.driade.com

Edra
www.edra.com

Fornasetti
www.fornasetti.com

Friedman Benda
515 West 26th Street
New York, NY 10001
USA
Tel. +1 (212) 239 8700
E-mail:
gallery@friedmanbenda.com
www.friedmanbenda.com

Fritz Hansen
www.fritzhansen.com

Heller
www.helleronline.com

Knoll
www.knoll.com

Lusty Furniture Co. Ltd
Cotswold Innovation Centre
42 Ellis Road
Rissington Business Park
Gloucestershire, GL54 2QB
Tel. +44 (0)1386 898010
www.lloydloomonline.com

Macklowe Gallery
667 Madison Avenue
New York, NY 10065
USA
Tel. +1 (212) 644 6400
E-mail:
email@MackloweGallery.com
www.macklowegallery.com

Graham Mancha Ltd
43 High Street, Wing
Bedfordshire LU7 0NS
UK
www.mancha.demon.co.uk

One Collection
www.onecollection.com

Partridge Fine Arts Ltd
144–146 New Bond Street
London W1S 2PF
UK
Tel. +44 (0)20 7629 0834
E-mail:
enquiries@partridgefineart.com
www.partridgefineart.com

Peter-Roberts 20th C. Design
Center 44, 222 East 44th Street
New York, NY 10017
US
Tel. +1 (212) 450 7988
E-mail: staff@center44.com
http://center44.com

R 20th Century Design
82 Franklin Street
New York, NY 10013
US
Tel. +1 (212) 343 7979
E-mail: r@r20thcentury.com
www.r20thcentury.com

SCP
135–139 Curtain Road
London EC2A 3BX
UK
www.scp.co.uk

David J Shuttleton
The Chairman of Bearsden
974 Pollokshaws Road
Glasgow G41 2HA
UK
Tel. +44 (0)141 639 5830

Vitra
www.vitra.com

Witney Antiques
96–100 Corn Street
Witney
Oxfordshire OX28 6BU
UK
Tel. +44 (0)1993 370 3902
E-mail:
witneyantiques@community.co.uk
www.witneyantiques.com

Wittmann
www.wittmann.at

The author would like to thank...

Many people have fuelled my passion for chairs, not least my husband John Wainwright, although he has often maintained that 'we do not need one more single chair' – a somewhat mystifying concept. Many people have helped bring this project to fruition. Friends have been generous with sharing their visions, ideas, contacts and knowledge, in particular Gloria Stewart, Diane Pease, and Fayal Greene. I would like to give enormous thanks to the Conran team: Lorraine Dickey for her enthusiasm and commitment, Jonathan Christie for his inspirational design, Sybella Marlow for her patience and encouragement and Alison Wormleighton for her perceptive queries and incisive comment. Also Anne-Marie Hoines for her hard work, inspired locations and her dogged determination to track down recalcitrant chairs and Matt Riches, Nu-Nu Yee Hoggarth and Jonathan Bird for organizing the shoots. Most importantly also thanks to Nick Pope for his quite spectacular photography and understanding of the project.

A big thank you to Terence & Vicki Conran for letting us shoot their chairs and use their houses. Sophie at Light Locations who helped source locations, John and Genevieve Christie for letting us shoot their chairs and cat (Fluffy) in their barn, Penny at Tattersall-Love, Richard Clatworthy and Heather Lewin.

Many thanks for the advice and contribution from John Bly of Tring, Mark Law of Partridge Fine Art, Zesty Meyers and Evan Snyderman of R20th Century, David Rago of The Rago Arts & Auction Center, Peter Roberts of Peter Roberts Antiques, Jennifer Olshin at Friedman Benda, Dean Levy at Bernard & S. Dean Levy and Benjamin Macklowe at Macklowe Gallery.

Thanks also to the writers who contributed to the book: Marc Allum, Jill Bace, Keith Baker, John Bly, Julie and Nick Goodman, Albert Hill, Zesty Meyers, Alycen Mitchell, Jennifer Olshin, Jeremy Smith and Anna Southgate.

Judith Miller began collecting antiques in the 1960s while a student at Edinburgh University. Fascinated by the inexpensive plates she bought in the city's junk shops she began to research their history in books and auction catalogues. She has since become one of the world's leading experts in antiques. From 1979 until 1988, Judith served as co-founder of the international best-selling *Miller's Antiques Price Guide* and has since written more than 80 books, many of which are held in high regard by collectors and dealers. Judith is a regular lecturer and contributor to numerous newspapers and magazines, including *BBC Homes & Antiques* and *House & Garden*, and appears regularly on radio and TV, most notably as co-host for the popular BBC series *The House Detectives* and is an expert on the BBC *Antiques Roadshow*. She regularly lectures in the US to Art & Antiques Charity events and is a regular lecturer to Appraisers societies, the AAA in New York and recently the IAS in Fort Worth Texas. Twice a year she does an antiques lecture tour of the US with associated TV, radio and press.

Nick Pope started taking pictures aged 8 when he was given a light meter and twenty rolls of out of date film. He's still gripped 35 years later. After studying furniture design for three years at Ravensbourne College, he returned to his original love of photography, where he has since found his perfect balance photographing interiors and furniture for a wide range of international clients. His work has appeared in *House & Garden*, *Harpers & Queen*, *Elle Decoration*, *Red* and *Gourmet*. He lives in North London with Sammie his wife, their two children Jim & Iris, and a Cherner chair. 'The chairs were perfect subjects. Languid and beautiful, often eccentric and loads of attitude… and there was always somewhere to sit.'